1542. Birth of Juan de Yepes at Fontiveros, near Ávila. The day generally ascribed to this event is June 24.

1543 (?). Death of Juan's father.

1552–6 (?). Juan goes to school at the Colegio de los Niños de la Doctrina, Medina.

1556–7. Don Antonio Álvarez de Toledo takes Juan into a Hospital to train him for Holy Orders under his patronage.

1559–63 (?). Juan attends the Jesuit College at Medina.

1562. Leaves the Hospital and the patronage of Álvarez de Toledo.

1563. Takes the Carmelite habit at St. Anne's, Medina del Campo, as Juan de San Matías (Santo Matía).

1564–5. Makes his profession. (November). Enters the University of Salamanca. (January 6). Matriculates.

1567. Receives priest's orders (probably in the summer).

1567. (September ?). Meets St. Teresa at Medina del Campo and agrees to join her Discalced Reform.

1568 (November 28). Takes the vows of the Reform at Duruelo as St. John of the Cross, together with Antonio de Heredia (Antonio de Jesús), Prior of the Calced Carmelites at Medina, and José de Cristo, another Carmelite from Medina.

1571. (April ?). Goes to Alcalá de Henares as Rector of the College of the Reform and directs the Carmelite nuns.

1572 (shortly after April 23). Recalled to Pastrana to correct the rigours of the new novice-master.

1572. Goes to Ávila as confessor to the Convent of the Incarnation. Remains there till 1577.

1575–6 (Winter of: before February 1576). Kidnapped by the Calced and imprisoned at Medina del Campo. Freed by the intervention of the Papal Nuncio, Ormaneto.

1577 (December 2 or 3). Kidnapped by the Calced and imprisoned in the Calced Carmelite priory at Toledo.

1577–8. Composes in prison 17 (or 30) stanzas of the 'Spiritual Canticle': the poem with the refrain 'Although 'tis night'; and the stanzas beginning 'In principio erat verbum.'

1578 (August 16 or shortly afterwards). Escapes to the Convent of the Carmelite nuns in Toledo.

1578 (October 9). Attends a meeting of the Discalced superiors at Almodovar. Is sent to El Calvario as Vicar.

1579 (June 14). Founds a college of the Reform at Baeza.

1579–82. Resides at Baeza as Rector of the college.

1580. Death of his mother.

1581 (March 3). Attends the Álcala Chapter of the Reform. Appointed Third Definitor and Prior of the Granada house of Los Mártires.

1581 (November 28). Last meeting with St. Teresa, at Ávila.

1582–8. Re-elected (or confirmed) as Prior of Los Mártires, 1583. Resides at Los Mártires more or less continuously till 1584 and intermittently afterwards; finishes the *Ascent of Mount Carmel* there and composes his remaining prose treatises. Writes *Living Flame of Love* about 1585, in fifteen days.

1585 (May). Lisbon Chapter appoints him Second Definitor and (ill 1587) Vicar-Provincial of Andalusia. Makes the following foundations: Málaga, 1585; Córdoba, La Manchuela (de Jaén), Caravaca, 1586; Bujalance, 1587.

1587 (April). Chapter of Valladolid re-appoints him Prior of Los Mártires. He ceases to be Definitor and Vicar-Provincial.

1588 (June 19). Attends first Chapter-General of the Reform in Madrid. Elected First Definitor and *consiliario*.

1588 (August 10). Becomes Prior of Segovia.

1590 (June 10). Re-elected First Definitor and *consiliario*.

1591 (June 1). The Madrid Chapter-General deprives him of his offices and resolves to send him to Mexico. (This latter decision was later revoked.)

1591 (December 14). Dies at Úbeda.

January 25, 1675. Beatified by Clement X.

December 26, 1726. Canonized by Benedict XIII.

August 24, 1926. Declared Doctor of the Church Universal by Pius XI.

DARK NIGHT
OF THE SOUL

by

Saint John of the Cross
DOCTOR OF THE CHURCH

THIRD REVISED EDITION

Translated and edited, with an Introduction,
by E. ALLISON PEERS
from the critical edition of
P. SILVERIO DE SANTA TERESA, C.D.

IMAGE BOOKS

A Division of Doubleday & Company, Inc.
Garden City, New York

IMAGE BOOKS EDITION 1959
by special arrangement with The Newman Press

Image Books edition published February 1959

COVER BY WILLIAM MEEK
TYPOGRAPHY BY JOSEPH P. ASCHERL
Printed in the United States of America

CONTENTS

DARK NIGHT OF THE SOUL

BOOK I

BOOK II

TRANSLATOR'S PREFACE
TO THE FIRST EDITION

I

FOR at least twenty years, a new translation of the works of
St. John of the Cross has been an urgent necessity. The
translations of the individual prose works now in general use
go back in their original form to the eighteen-sixties, and,
though the later editions of some of them have been sub-
mitted to a certain degree of revision, nothing but a complete
retranslation of the works from their original Spanish could
be satisfactory. For this there are two reasons.

First, the existing translations were never very exact renderings of the original Spanish text even in the form which
held the field when they were first published. Their great
merit was extreme readableness: many a disciple of the Spanish mystics, who is unacquainted with the language in which
they wrote, owes to these translations the comparative ease
with which he has mastered the main lines of St. John of the
Cross's teaching. Thus for the general reader they were of
great utility; for the student, on the other hand, they have
never been entirely adequate. They paraphrase difficult expressions, omit or add to parts of individual sentences in order
(as it seems) to facilitate comprehension of the general drift
of the passages in which these occur, and frequently retrans-
late from the Vulgate the Saint's Spanish quotations from
Holy Scripture instead of turning into English the quotations
themselves, using the text actually before them.

A second and more important reason for a new translation,
however, is the discovery of fresh manuscripts and the con-
sequent improvements which have been made in the Spanish
text of the works of St. John of the Cross, during the present
century. Seventy years ago, the text chiefly used was that of

the collection known as the *Biblioteca de Autores Españoles* (1853), which itself was based, as we shall later see, upon an edition going back as far as 1703, published before modern methods of editing were so much as imagined. Both the text of the *B.A.E.* edition and the unimportant commentary which accompanied it were highly unsatisfactory, yet until the beginning of the present century nothing appreciably better was attempted.

In the last twenty years, however, we have had two new editions, each based upon a close study of the extant manuscripts and each representing a great advance upon the editions preceding it. The three-volume Toledo edition of P. Gerardo de San Juan de la Cruz, C.D. (1912–14), was the first attempt made to produce an accurate text by modern critical methods. Its execution was perhaps less laudable than its conception, and faults were pointed out in it from the time of its appearance, but it served as a new starting-point for Spanish scholars and stimulated them to a new interest in St. John of the Cross's writings. Then, seventeen years later, came the magnificent five-volume edition of P. Silverio de Santa Teresa, C.D. (Burgos, 1929–31), which forms the basis of this present translation. So superior is it, even on the most casual examination, to all its predecessors that to eulogize it in detail is superfluous. It is founded upon a larger number of texts than has previously been known and it collates them with greater skill than that of any earlier editor. It can hardly fail to be the standard edition of the works of St. John of the Cross for generations.

Thanks to the labours of these Carmelite scholars and of others whose findings they have incorporated in their editions, Spanish students can now approach the work of the great Doctor with the reasonable belief that they are reading, as nearly as may be, what he actually wrote. English-reading students, however, who are unable to master sixteenth-century Spanish, have hitherto had no grounds for such a belief. They cannot tell whether, in any particular passage, they are face to face with the Saint's own words, with a translator's free paraphrase of them or with a gloss made by some later copyist or early editor in the supposed interests of orthodoxy.

Indeed, they cannot be sure that some whole paragraph is not one of the numerous interpolations which has its rise in an early printed edition—i.e., the timorous qualifications of statements which have seemed to the interpolator over-bold. Even some of the most distinguished writers in English on St. John of the Cross have been misled in this way and it has been impossible for any but those who read Spanish with ease to make a systematic and reliable study of such an important question as the alleged dependence of Spanish quietists upon the Saint, while his teaching on the mystical life has quite unwittingly been distorted by persons who would least wish to misrepresent it in any particular.

It was when writing the chapter on St. John of the Cross in the first volume of my *Studies of the Spanish Mystics* (in which, as it was published in 1927, I had not the advantage of using P. Silverio's edition) that I first realized the extent of the harm caused by the lack of an accurate and modern translation. Making my own versions of all the passages quoted, I had sometimes occasion to compare them with those of other translators, which at their worst were almost unrecognizable as versions of the same originals. Then and there I resolved that, when time allowed, I would make a fresh translation of the works of a saint to whom I have long had great devotion—to whom, indeed, I owe more than to any other writer outside the Scriptures. Just at that time I happened to visit the Discalced Carmelites at Burgos, where I first met P. Silverio, and found, to my gratification, that his edition of St. John of the Cross was much nearer publication than I had imagined. Arrangements for sole permission to translate the new edition were quickly made and work on the early volumes was begun even before the last volume was published.

II

These preliminary notes will explain why my chief preoccupation throughout the performance of this task has been to present as accurate and reliable a version of St. John of the Cross's works as it is possible to obtain. To keep the translation, line by line, *au pied de la lettre*, is, of course, impracticable: and such constantly occurring Spanish habits as the use of abstract nouns in the plural and the verbal construction 'ir + present participle' introduce shades of meaning which cannot always be reproduced. Yet wherever, for stylistic or other reasons, I have departed from the Spanish in any way that could conceivably cause a misunderstanding, I have scrupulously indicated this in a footnote. Further, I have translated, not only the text, but the variant readings as given by P. Silverio,[1] except where they are due merely to slips of the copyist's pen or where they differ so slightly from the readings of the text that it is impossible to render the differences in English. I beg students not to think that some of the smaller changes noted are of no importance; closer examination will often show that, however slight they may seem, they are, in relation to their context, or to some particular aspect of the Saint's teaching, of real interest; in other places they help to give the reader an idea, which may be useful to him in some crucial passage, of the general characteristics of the mauscript or edition in question. The editor's notes on the manuscripts and early editions which he has collated will also be found, for the same reason, to be summarized in the introduction to each work; in consulting the variants, the English-reading student has the maximum aid to a judgment of the reliability of his authorities.

Concentration upon the aim of obtaining the most precise possible rendering of the text has led me to sacrifice stylistic elegance to exactness where the two have been in conflict; it has sometimes been difficult to bring oneself to reproduce the Saint's often ungainly, though often forceful, repetitions of words or his long, cumbrous parentheses, but the temptation to take refuge in graceful paraphrases has been steadily resisted. In the same interest, and also in that of space, I have made certain omissions from, and abbreviations of, other parts of the edition than the text. Two of P. Silverio's five volumes are entirely filled with commentaries and documents. I have selected from the documents those of outstanding interest to readers with no detailed knowledge of

[1] The footnotes are P. Silverio's except where they are enclosed in square brackets.

Spanish religious history and have been content to summarize the editor's introductions to the individual works, as well as his longer footnotes to the text, and to omit such parts as would interest only specialists, who are able, or at least should be obliged, to study them in the original Spanish.

The decision to summarize in these places has been made the less reluctantly because of the frequent unsuitability of P. Silverio's style to English readers. Like that of many Spaniards, it is so discursive, and at times so baroque in its wealth of epithet and its profusion of imagery, that a literal translation, for many pages together, would seldom have been acceptable. The same criticism would have been applicable to any literal translation of P. Silverio's biography of St. John of the Cross which stands at the head of his edition (Vol. I, pp. 7–130). There was a further reason for omitting these biographical chapters. The long and fully documented biography by the French Carmelite, P. Bruno de Jésus-Marie, C.D., written from the same standpoint as P. Silverio's, has recently been translated into English, and any attempt to rival this in so short a space would be foredoomed to failure. I have thought, however, that a brief outline of the principal events in St. John of the Cross's life would be a useful preliminary to this edition; this has therefore been substituted for the biographical sketch referred to.

In language, I have tried to reproduce the atmosphere of a sixteenth-century text as far as is consistent with clarity. Though following the paragraph divisions of my original, I have not scrupled, where this has seemed to facilitate understanding, to divide into shorter sentences the long and sometimes straggling periods in which the Saint so frequently indulged. Some attempt has been made to show the contrast between the highly adorned, poetical language of much of the commentary on the 'Spiritual Canticle' and the more closely shorn and eminently practical, though always somewhat discursive style of the *Ascent* and *Dark Night*. That the *Living Flame* occupies an intermediate position in this respect should also be clear from the style of the translation.

Quotations, whether from the Scriptures or from other sources, have been left strictly as St. John of the Cross made them. Where he quotes in Latin, the Latin has been reproduced; only his quotations in Spanish have been turned into English. The footnote references are to the Vulgate, of which the Douai Version is a direct translation; if the Authorized Version differs, as in the Psalms, the variation has been shown in square brackets for the convenience of those who use it.

A word may not be out of place regarding the translations of the poems as they appear in the prose commentaries. Obviously, it would have been impossible to use the comparatively free verse renderings which appear in Volume II of this translation, since the commentaries discuss each line and often each word of the poems. A literal version of the poems in their original verse-lines, however, struck me as being inartistic, if not repellent, and as inviting continual comparison with the more polished verse renderings which, in spirit, come far nearer to the poet's aim. My first intention was to translate the poems, for the purpose of the commentaries, into prose. But later I hit upon the long and metrically unfettered verse-line, suggestive of Biblical poetry in its English dress, which I have employed throughout. I believe that, although the renderings often suffer artistically from their necessary literalness, they are from the artistic standpoint at least tolerable.

III

The debts I have to acknowledge, though few, are very large ones. My gratitude to P. Silverio de Santa Teresa for telling me so much about his edition before its publication, granting my publishers the sole translation rights and discussing with me a number of crucial passages cannot be disjoined from the many kindnesses I have received during my work on the Spanish mystics, which is still proceeding, from himself and from his fellow-Carmelites in the province of Castile. In dedicating this translation to them, I think particularly of P. Silverio in Burgos, of P. Florencio del Niño Jesús in Madrid, and of P. Crisógono de Jesús Sacramentado, together with the Fathers of the 'Convento de la Santa' in Ávila.

The long and weary process of revising the manuscript and proofs of this translation has been greatly lightened by the co-operation and companionship of P. Edmund Gurdon, Prior of the Cartuja de Miraflores, near Burgos, with whom I have freely discussed all kinds of difficulties, both of substance and style, and who has been good enough to read part of my proofs. From the quiet library of his monastery, as well as from his gracious companionship, I have drawn not only knowledge, but strength, patience and perseverance. And when at length, after each of my visits, we have had to part, we have continued our labours by correspondence, shaking hands, as it were, 'over a vast' and embracing 'from the ends of opposèd winds.'

Finally, I owe a real debt to my publishers for allowing me to do this work without imposing any such limitations of time as often accompany literary undertakings. This and other considerations which I have received from them have made that part of the work which has been done outside the study unusually pleasant and I am correspondingly grateful.

E. ALLISON PEERS.

UNIVERSITY OF LIVERPOOL.
Feast of St. John of the Cross,
November 24, 1933.

NOTE.—Wherever a commentary by St. John of the Cross is referred to, its title is given in italics (e.g. *Spiritual Canticle*); where the corresponding poem is meant, it is placed between quotation marks (e.g. 'Spiritual Canticle'). The abbreviation 'e.p.' stands for *editio princeps* throughout.

TRANSLATOR'S PREFACE
TO THE SECOND EDITION

DURING the sixteen years which have elapsed since the
publication of the first edition, several reprints have been
issued, and the demand is now such as to justify a complete
resetting. I have taken advantage of this opportunity to re-
vise the text throughout, and hope that in some of the more
difficult passages I may have come nearer than before to the
Saint's mind. Recent researches have necessitated a considerable amplification of introductions and footnotes and
greatly increased the length of the bibliography.

The only modification which has been made consistently
throughout the three volumes relates to St. John of the
Cross's quotations from Scripture. In translating these I still
follow him exactly, even where he himself is inexact, but I
have used the Douai Version (instead of the Authorized, as
in the first edition) as a basis for all Scriptural quotations, as
well as in the footnote references and the Scriptural index in
Vol. III.

Far more is now known of the life and times of St. John of
the Cross than when this translation of the *Complete Works*
was first published, thanks principally to the *Historia del
Carmen Descalzo* of P. Silverio de Santa Teresa, C.D., now
General of his Order, and to the admirably documented Life
of the Saint written by P. Crisógono de Jesús Sacramentado,
C.D., and published (in *Vida y Obras de San Juan de la
Cruz*) in the year after his untimely death. This increased
knowledge is reflected in many additional notes, and also in
the 'Outline of the Life of St. John of the Cross' (Vol. I,
pp. xxv–xxviii), which, for this edition, has been entirely
recast. References are given to my *Handbook to the Life and
Times of St. Teresa and St. John of the Cross*, which provides
much background too full to be reproduced in footnotes and

too complicated to be compressed. The *Handbook* also contains numerous references to contemporary events, omitted from the 'Outline' as being too remote from the main theme to justify inclusion in a summary necessarily so condensed.

My thanks for help in revision are due to kindly correspondents, too numerous to name, from many parts of the world, who have made suggestions for the improvement of the first edition; to the Rev. Professor David Knowles, of Cambridge University, for whose continuous practical interest in this translation I cannot be too grateful; to Miss I. L. McClelland, of Glasgow University, who has read a large part of this edition in proof; to Dom Philippe Chevallier, for material which I have been able to incorporate in it; to P. José Antonio de Sobrino, S.J., for allowing me to quote freely from his recently published *Estudios*; and, most of all, to M. R. P. Silverio de Santa Teresa, C.D., and the Fathers of the International Carmelite College at Rome, whose learning and experience, are, I hope, faintly reflected in this new edition.

E. A. P.

June 30, 1951.

PRINCIPAL ABBREVIATIONS

A.V.—Authorized Version of the Bible (1611).

D.V.—Douai Version of the Bible (1609).

C.W.S.T.J.—*The Complete Works of Saint Teresa of Jesus,* translated and edited by E. Allison Peers from the critical edition of P. Silverio de Santa Teresa, C.D. London, Sheed and Ward, 1946. 3 vols.

H.—E. Allison Peers: *Handbook to the Life and Times of St. Teresa and St. John of the Cross.* London, Burns Oates and Washbourne, 1953.

LL.—*The Letters of Saint Teresa of Jesus,* translated and edited by E. Allison Peers from the critical edition of P. Silverio de Santa Teresa, C.D. London, Burns Oates and Washbourne, 1951. 2 vols.

N.L.M.—National Library of Spain (Biblioteca Nacional), Madrid.

Obras (P. Silv.)—*Obras de San Juan de la Cruz,* Doctor de la Iglesia, editadas y anotadas por el P. Silverio de Santa Teresa, C.D. Burgos, 1929–31. 5 vols.

S.S.M.—E. Allison Peers: *Studies of the Spanish Mystics.* Vol. I, London, Sheldon Press, 1927; 2nd ed., London, S.P.C.K., 1951. Vol. II, London, Sheldon Press, 1930.

Sobrino.—José Antonio de Sobrino, S.J.: *Estudios sobre San Juan de la Cruz y nuevos textos de su obra.* Madrid, 1950.

DARK NIGHT OF THE SOUL

INTRODUCTION

SOMEWHAT reluctantly, out of respect for a venerable tradition, we publish the *Dark Night* as a separate treatise, though in reality it is a continuation of the *Ascent of Mount Carmel* and fulfils the undertakings given in it:

The first night or purgation is of the sensual part of the soul, which is treated in the present stanza, and will be treated in the first part of this book. And the second is of the spiritual part; of this speaks the second stanza, which follows; and of this we shall treat likewise, in the second and the third part, with respect to the activity of the soul; *and in the fourth part, with respect to its passivity.*[1]

This 'fourth part' is the *Dark Night*. Of it the Saint writes in a passage which follows that just quoted:

And the second night, or purification, pertains to those who are already proficient, occurring at the time when God desires to bring them to the state of union with God. And this latter night is a more obscure and dark and terrible purgation, as we shall say afterwards.[2]

In his three earlier books he has written of the Active Night, of Sense and of Spirit; he now proposes to deal with the Passive Night, in the same order. He has already taught us how we are to deny and purify ourselves with the ordinary help of grace, in order to prepare our senses and faculties for union with God through love. He now proceeds to explain, with an arresting freshness, how these same senses and faculties are purged and purified by God with a view to the same

[1] *Ascent*, Bk. I, chap. i, § 2. Cf. p. 2, above.
[2] *Op. cit.*, § 3.

end—that of union. The combined description of the two nights completes the presentation of active and passive purgation, to which the Saint limits himself in these treatises, although the subject of the stanzas which he is glossing is a much wider one, comprising the whole of the mystical life and ending only with the Divine embraces of the soul transformed in God through love.

The stanzas expounded by the Saint are taken from the same poem in the two treatises. The commentary upon the second, however, is very different from that upon the first, for it assumes a much more advanced state of development. The Active Night has left the senses and faculties well prepared, though not completely prepared, for the reception of Divine influences and illuminations in greater abundance than before. The Saint here postulates a principle of dogmatic theology—that by himself, and with the ordinary aid of grace, man cannot attain to that degree of purgation which is essential to his transformation in God. He needs Divine aid more abundantly. 'However greatly the soul itself labours,' writes the Saint, 'it cannot actively purify itself so as to be in the least degree prepared for the Divine union of perfection of love, if God takes not its hand and purges it not in that dark fire.'[3]

The Passive Nights, in which it is God Who accomplishes the purgation, are based upon this incapacity. Souls 'begin to enter' this dark night

when God draws them forth from the state of beginners—which is the state of those that meditate on the spiritual road—and begins to set them in the state of progressives—which is that of those who are already contemplatives—to the end that, after passing through it, they may arrive at the state of the perfect, which is that of the Divine union of the soul with God.[4]

Before explaining the nature and effects of this Passive Night, the Saint touches, in passing, upon certain imperfections found in those who are about to enter it and which it removes

[3] *Dark Night*, Bk. I, chap. iii, § 3.
[4] *Op. cit.*, Bk. I, chap. i, § 1.

by the process of purgation. Such travellers are still untried proficients, who have not yet acquired mature habits of spirituality and who therefore still conduct themselves as children. The imperfections are examined one by one, following the order of the seven deadly sins, in chapters (ii–viii) which once more reveal the author's skill as a director of souls. They are easy chapters to understand, and of great practical utility, comparable to those in the first book of the *Ascent* which deal with the active purgation of the desires of sense.

In Chapter viii, St. John of the Cross begins to describe the Passive Night of the senses, the principal aim of which is the purgation or stripping of the soul of its imperfections and the preparation of it for fruitive union. The Passive Night of Sense, we are told, is 'common' and 'comes to many,' whereas that of Spirit 'is the portion of very few.'[5] The one is 'bitter and terrible' but 'the second bears no comparison with it,' for it is 'horrible and awful to the spirit.'[6] A good deal of literature on the former Night existed in the time of St. John of the Cross and he therefore promises to be brief in his treatment of it. Of the latter, on the other hand, he will 'treat more fully . . . since very little has been said of this, either in speech or in writing, and very little is known of it, even by experience.'[7]

Having described this Passive Night of Sense in Chapter viii, he explains with great insight and discernment how it may be recognized whether any given aridity is a result of this Night or whether it comes from sins or imperfections, or from frailty or lukewarmness of spirit, or even from indisposition or 'humours' of the body. The Saint is particularly effective here, and we may once more compare this chapter with a similar one in the *Ascent* (II, xiii)—that in which he fixes the point where the soul may abandon discursive meditation and enter the contemplation which belongs to loving and simple faith.

Both these chapters have contributed to the reputation of St. John of the Cross as a consummate spiritual master. And

[5] *Dark Night*, Bk. I, chap. viii, § 1.
[6] *Op. cit.*, Bk. I, chap. viii, § 2.
[7] *Ibid.*

this not only for the objective value of his observations, but because, even in spite of himself, he betrays the sublimity of his own mystical experiences. Once more, too, we may admire the crystalline transparency of his teaching and the precision of the phrases in which he clothes it. To judge by his language alone, one might suppose at times that he is speaking of mathematical, rather than of spiritual operations.

In Chapter x, the Saint describes the discipline which the soul in this Dark Night must impose upon itself; this, as might be logically deduced from the *Ascent,* consists in 'allowing the soul to remain in peace and quietness,' content 'with a peaceful and loving attentiveness toward God.'[8] Before long it will experience enkindlings of love (Chapter xi), which will serve to purify its sins and imperfections and draw it gradually nearer to God; we have here, as it were, so many stages of the ascent of the Mount on whose summit the soul attains to transforming union. Chapters xii and xiii detail with great exactness the benefits that the soul receives from this aridity, while Chapter xiv briefly expounds the last line of the first stanza and brings to an end what the Saint desires to say with respect to the first Passive Night.

At only slightly greater length St. John of the Cross describes the Passive Night of the Spirit, which is at once more afflictive and more painful than those which have preceded it. This, nevertheless, is the Dark Night *par excellence,* of which the Saint speaks in these words: 'The night which we have called that of sense may and should be called a kind of correction and restraint of the desire rather than purgation. The reason is that all the imperfections and disorders of the sensual part have their strength and root in the spirit, where all habits, both good and bad, are brought into subjection, and thus, until these are purged, the rebellions and depravities of sense cannot be purged thoroughly.'[9]

Spiritual persons, we are told, do not enter the second night immediately after leaving the first; on the contrary, they generally pass a long time, even years, before doing so,[10]

[8] *Dark Night,* Bk. I, chap. x, § 4.
[9] *Op. cit.,* Bk. II, chap. iii, § 1.
[10] *Op. cit.,* Bk. II, chap. i, § 1.

for they still have many imperfections, both habitual and actual (Chapter ii). After a brief introduction (Chapter iii), the Saint describes with some fullness the nature of this spiritual purgation or dark contemplation referred to in the first stanza of his poem and the varieties of pain and affliction caused by it, whether in the soul or in its faculties (Chapters iv–viii). These chapters are brilliant beyond all description; in them we seem to reach the culminating point of their author's mystical experience; any excerpt from them would do them an injustice. It must suffice to say that St. John of the Cross seldom again touches those same heights of sublimity.

Chapter ix describes how, although these purgations seem to blind the spirit, they do so only to enlighten it again with a brighter and intenser light, which it is preparing itself to receive with greater abundance. The following chapter makes the comparison between spiritual purgation and the log of wood which gradually becomes transformed through being immersed in fire and at last takes on the fire's own properties. The force with which the familiar similitude is driven home impresses indelibly upon the mind the fundamental concept of this most sublime of all purgations. Marvellous, indeed, are its effects, from the first enkindlings and burnings of Divine love, which are greater beyond comparison than those produced by the Night of Sense, the one being as different from the other as is the body from the soul. 'For this (latter) is an enkindling of spiritual love in the soul, which, in the midst of these dark confines, feels itself to be keenly and sharply wounded in strong Divine love, and to have a certain realization and foretaste of God.'[11] No less wonderful are the effects of the powerful Divine illumination which from time to time enfolds the soul in the splendours of glory. When the effects of the light that wounds and yet illumines are combined with those of the enkindlement that melts the soul with its heat, the delights experienced are so great as to be ineffable.

The second line of the first stanza of the poem is expounded in three admirable chapters (xi–xiii), while one short chapter

[11] *Dark Night*, Bk. II, chap. xi, § 1.

(xiv) suffices for the three lines remaining. We then embark upon the second stanza, which describes the soul's security in the Dark Night—due, among other reasons, to its being freed 'not only from itself, but likewise from its other enemies, which are the world and the devil.'[12]

This contemplation is not only dark, but also secret (Chapter xvii), and in Chapter xviii is compared to the 'staircase' of the poem. This comparison suggests to the Saint an exposition (Chapters xviii, xix) of the ten steps or degrees of love which comprise St. Bernard's mystical ladder. Chapter xxi describes the soul's 'disguise,' from which the book passes on (Chapters xxii, xxiii) to extol the 'happy chance' which led it to journey 'in darkness and concealment' from its enemies, both without and within.

Chapter xxiv glosses the last line of the second stanza— 'my house being now at rest.' Both the higher and the lower 'portions of the soul' are now tranquillized and prepared for the desired union with the Spouse, a union which is the subject that the Saint proposed to treat in his commentary on the five remaining stanzas. As far as we know, this commentary was never written. We have only the briefest outline of what was to have been covered in the third, in which, following the same effective metaphor of night, the Saint describes the excellent properties of the spiritual night of infused contemplation, through which the soul journeys with no other guide or support, either outward or inward, than the Divine love 'which burned in my heart.'

It is difficult to express adequately the sense of loss that one feels at the premature truncation of this eloquent treatise.[13] We have already given our opinion[14] upon the commentaries thought to have been written on the final stanzas of the 'Dark Night.' Did we possess them, they would explain the birth of the light—'dawn's first breathings in the heav'ns above'—which breaks through the black darkness of the Active and the Passive Nights; they would tell us, too, of the

---

[12] *Dark Night*, Bk. II, chap. xvi, § 2.
[13] [On this, see Sobrino, pp. 159–66.]
[14] Cf. pp. lviii–lxiii, *Ascent of Mount Carmel* (Image Books edition).

soul's further progress towards the Sun's full brightness. It is true, of course, that some part of this great gap is filled by St. John of the Cross himself in his other treatises, but it is small compensation for the incomplete state in which he left this edifice of such gigantic proportions that he should have given us other and smaller buildings of a somewhat similar kind. Admirable as are the *Spiritual Canticle* and the *Living Flame of Love*, they are not so completely knit into one whole as is this great double treatise. They lose both in flexibility and in substance through the closeness with which they follow the stanzas of which they are the exposition. In the *Ascent* and the *Dark Night*, on the other hand, we catch only the echoes of the poem, which are all but lost in the resonance of the philosopher's voice and the eloquent tones of the preacher. Nor have the other treatises the learning and the authority of these. Nowhere else does the genius of St. John of the Cross for infusing philosophy into his mystical dissertations find such an outlet as here. Nowhere else, again, is he quite so appealingly human; for, though he is human even in his loftiest and sublimest passages, this intermingling of philosophy with mystical theology makes him seem particularly so. These treatises are a wonderful illustration of the theological truth that grace, far from destroying nature, ennobles and dignifies it, and of the agreement always found between the natural and the supernatural—between the principles of sound reason and the sublimest manifestations of Divine grace.

Manuscripts of the *DARK NIGHT*

The autograph of the *Dark Night*, like that of the *Ascent of Mount Carmel*, is unknown to us: the second seems to have disappeared in the same period as the first. There are extant, however, as many as twelve early copies of the *Dark Night*, some of which, though none of them is as palæographically accurate as the best copy of the *Ascent*, are very reliable; there is no trace in them of conscious adulteration of the original or of any kind of modification to fit the sense of any passage into a preconceived theory. We definitely prefer one of these copies to the others but we nowhere follow it so literally as to incorporate in our text its evident discrepancies from its original.

MS. 3,446. An early MS. in the clear masculine hand of an Andalusian: MS. 3,446 in the National Library, Madrid. Like many others, this MS. was transferred to the library from the Convento de San Hermenegildo at the time of the religious persecutions in the early nineteenth century; it had been presented to the Archives of the Reform by the Fathers of Los Remedios, Seville—a Carmelite house founded by P. Gracián in 1574. It has no title and a fragment from the *Living Flame of Love* is bound up with it.

This MS. has only two omissions of any length; these form part respectively of Book II, Chapters xix and xxiii, dealing with the Passive Night of the Spirit. It has many copyist's errors. At the same time, its antiquity and origin, and the good faith of which it shows continual signs, give it, in our view, primacy over the other copies now to come under consideration. It must be made clear, nevertheless, that there is no extant copy of the *Dark Night* as trustworthy and as skilfully made as the Alcaudete MS. of the *Ascent*.

MS. of the Carmelite Nuns of Toledo. Written in three hands, all early. Save for a few slips of the copyist, it agrees with the foregoing; a few of its errors have been corrected. It bears no title, but has a long sub-title which is in effect a partial summary of the argument.

MS. of the Carmelite Nuns of Valladolid. This famous convent, which was one of St. Teresa's foundations, is very rich in Teresan autographs, and has also a number of important documents relating to St. John of the Cross, together with some copies of his works. That here described is written in a large, clear hand and probably dates from the end of the sixteenth century. It has a title similar to that of the last-named copy. With few exceptions it follows the other most important MSS.

MS. Alba de Tormes. What has been said of this in the introduction to the *Ascent* (Image Books edition, pp. 6–7) applies also to the *Dark Night*. It is complete, save for small omissions on the part of the amanuensis, the 'Argument' at the beginning of the poem, the verses themselves and a few lines from Book II, Chapter vii.

MS. 6,624. This copy is almost identical with the foregoing. It omits the 'Argument' and the poem itself but not the lines from Book II, Chapter vii.

MS. 8,795. This contains the *Dark Night, Spiritual Canticle, Living Flame of Love*, a number of poems by St. John of the Cross and the *Spiritual Colloquies between Christ and the soul His Bride*. It is written in various hands, all very early and some feminine. A note by P. Andrés de la Encarnación, on the reverse of the first folio, records that the copy was presented to the Archives of the Reform by the Discalced Carmelite nuns of Baeza. This convent was founded in 1589, two years before the Saint's death, and the copy may well date from about this period. On the second folio comes the poem 'I entered in—I knew not where.' On the reverse of the third folio begins a kind of preface to the *Dark Night*, opening with the words: 'Begin the stanzas by means of which a soul may occupy itself and become fervent in the love of God. It deals with the Dark Night and is divided into two books. The first treats of the purgation of sense, and the second of the spiritual purgation of man. It was written by P. Fr. Juan de la Cruz, Discalced Carmelite.' On the next folio, a so-called 'Preface: To the Reader' begins: 'As a beginning and an explanation of these two purgations of the Dark Night which are to be expounded hereafter, this chapter will show how narrow is the path that leads to eternal life and how completely detached and disencumbered must be those that are to enter thereby.' This fundamental idea is developed for the space of two folios. There follows a sonnet on the *Dark Night*,[15] and immediately afterwards comes the text of the treatise.

The copy contains many errors, but its only omission is that of the last chapter. There is no trace in it of any attempt to

---

[15] [It contains a series of paradoxical statements, after the style of those in *Ascent*, Bk. I, chap. xiii, and is of no great literary merit. P. Silverio reproduces it in Spanish on p. 302 (note) of his first volume.]

modify its original; indeed, the very nature and number of the copyist's errors are a testimony to his good faith.

MS. 12,658. A note by P. Andrés states that he acquired it in Madrid but has no more detailed recollection of its *provenance*. 'The *Dark Night*,' it adds, 'begins on folio 43; our holy father is described simply as "the second friar of the new Reformation,"[16] which is clear evidence of its antiquity.'

The Codex contains a number of opuscules, transcribed no doubt with a devotional aim by the copyist. Its epoch is probably the end of the sixteenth century; it is certainly earlier than the editions. There is no serious omission except that of six lines of the 'Argument.' The authors of the other works copied include St. Augustine, B. Juan de Ávila, P. Baltasar Álvarez and P. Tomás de Jesús.

The copies which remain to be described are all mutilated or abbreviated and can be disposed of briefly:

MS. 13,498. This copy omits less of the *Dark Night* than of the *Ascent* but few pages are without their omissions. In one place a meticulous pair of scissors has removed the lower half of a folio on which the Saint deals with spiritual luxury.

MS. of the Carmelite Friars of Toledo. Dates from early in the seventeenth century and has numerous omissions, especially in the chapters on the Passive Night of the Spirit. The date is given (in the same hand as that which copies the title) as 1618. This MS. also contains an opuscule by Suso and another entitled 'Brief compendium of the most eminent Christian perfection of P. Fr. Juan de la Cruz.'

MS. 18,160. The copyist has treated the *Dark Night* little better than the *Ascent*; except from the first ten and the last three chapters, he omits freely.

MS. 12,411. Entitled by its copyist 'Spiritual Compendium,' this MS. contains several short works of devotion, including one by Ruysbroeck. Of St. John of the Cross's works it copies the *Spiritual Canticle* as well as the *Dark Night*;

[16] The 'first friar' would be P. Antonio de Jesús, who was senior to St. John of the Cross in the Carmelite Order, though not in the Reform.

the latter is headed: 'Song of one soul alone.' It also contains a number of poems, some of them by the Saint, and many passages from St. Teresa. It is in several hands, all of the seventeenth century. The copy of the *Dark Night* is most unsatisfactory; there are omissions and abbreviations everywhere.

M.S. of the Carmelite Nuns of Pamplona. This MS. also omits and abbreviates continually, especially in the chapters on the Passive Night of Sense, which are reduced to a mere skeleton.

Editio princeps. This is much more faithful to its original in the *Dark Night* than in the *Ascent*. Both the passages suppressed[17] and the interpolations[18] are relatively few and unimportant. Modifications of phraseology are more frequent and alterations are also made with the aim of correcting hyperbaton. In the first book about thirty lines are suppressed; in the second, about ninety. All changes which are of any importance have been shown in the notes.

The present edition. We have given preference, as a general rule, to MS. 3,446, subjecting it, however, to a rigorous comparison with the other copies. Mention has already been made in the introduction to the *Ascent* (Image Books edition, pp. lxiii–lxvi) of certain apparent anomalies and a certain lack of uniformity in the Saint's method of dividing his commentaries. This is nowhere more noticeable than in the *Dark Night*. Instead of dividing his treatise into books, each with its proper title, the Saint abandons this method and uses titles only occasionally. As this makes comprehension of his argument the more difficult, we have adopted the divisions which were introduced by P. Salablanca and have been copied by successive editors.

M. Baruzi (*Bulletin Hispanique*, 1922, Vol. xxiv, pp. 18–40) complains that this division weighs down the spiritual rhythm

---

[17] The longest of these are one of ten lines in Bk. I, chap. iv, [in the original] and those of Bk. II, chaps. vii, viii, xii, xiii, which vary from eleven to twenty-three lines. Bk. II, chap. xxiii, has also considerable modifications.

[18] The chief interpolation is in Bk. I, chap. x.

of the treatise and interrupts its movement. We do not agree. In any case, we greatly prefer the gain of clarity, even if the rhythm occasionally halts, to the other alternative—the constant halting of the understanding. We have, of course, indicated every place where the title is taken from the *editio princeps* and was not the work of the author.

The following abbreviations are adopted in the footnotes:

A = MS. of the Discalced Carmelite Friars of Alba.
B = MS. 6,624 (National Library, Madrid).
Bz. = MS. 8,795 (N.L.M.).
C = MS. 13,498 (N.L.M.).
G = MS. 18,160 (N.L.M.).
H = MS. 3,446 (N.L.M.).
M = MS. of the Discalced Carmelite Nuns of Toledo.
Mtr. = MS. 12,658.
P = MS. of the Discalced Carmelite Friars of Toledo.
V = MS. of the Discalced Carmelite Nuns of Valladolid.
E.p. = *Editio princeps* (1618).

MS. 12,411 and the MS. of the Discalced Carmelite nuns of Pamplona are cited without abbreviations.

DARK NIGHT[1]

Exposition of the stanzas describing the method followed by the soul in its journey upon the spiritual road to the attainment of the perfect union of love with God, to the extent that is possible in this life. Likewise are described the properties[2] belonging to the soul that has attained to the said perfection, according as they are contained in the same stanzas.[3]

PROLOGUE[4]

IN this book are first set down all the stanzas which are to be expounded; afterwards, each of the stanzas is expounded separately, being set down before its exposition; and then each line is expounded separately and in turn, the line itself also being set down before the exposition. In the first two stanzas are expounded the effects of the two spiritual purgations: of the sensual part of man and of the spiritual part. In the other six are expounded various and wondrous effects of the spiritual illumination and union of love with God.

STANZAS OF THE SOUL

1. On a dark night, Kindled in love with yearnings—oh, happy chance!—
   I went forth without being observed, My house being now at rest.

---

[1] This title is lacking in all the MSS. except Mtr. and P.

[2] C [incorrectly]: 'prosperities.'

[3] This sub-title is found in C, G, M, Mtr., which add some such words as 'by Fray Juan de la Cruz, Discalced Carmelite.' The *editio princeps* has both title and sub-title.

[4] So G, M. Bz. has 'Proem' and e.p. 'Argument.'

2. In darkness and secure, By the secret ladder, disguised—oh, happy chance!—
   In darkness and in concealment, My house being
   now at rest.

3. In the happy night, In secret, when none saw me,
   Nor I beheld aught, Without light or guide, save
   that which burned in my heart.

4. This light guided me More surely than the light
   of noonday
   To the place where he (well I knew who!) was
   awaiting me—
   A place where none appeared.

5. Oh, night that guided me, Oh, night more lovely
   than the dawn,
   Oh, night that joined Beloved with lover, Lover
   transformed in the Beloved!

6. Upon my flowery breast, Kept wholly for himself
   alone,
   There he stayed sleeping, and I caressed him, And
   the fanning of the cedars made a breeze.

7. The breeze blew from the turret As I parted his
   locks;
   With his gentle hand he wounded my neck And
   caused all my senses to be suspended.

8. I remained, lost in oblivion; My face I reclined on
   the Beloved.
   All ceased and I abandoned myself, Leaving my
   cares forgotten among the lilies.

Begins the exposition of the stanzas which treat of the way
and manner which the soul follows upon the road of the
union of love with God.[5]

[5] Thus H, M and other authorities. Some (including H) add the
author's name. Others omit the title. A, B have: 'Book the fifth of
the Dark Night.' E.p. has: 'Exposition of the intent of the Stanzas.'

Before we enter upon the exposition of these stanzas, it is well to understand here that the soul that utters them is now in the state of perfection, which is the union of love with God, having already passed through severe trials and straits, by means of spiritual exercise in the narrow way of eternal life whereof Our Saviour speaks in the Gospel, along which way the soul ordinarily passes in order to reach this high and happy union with God.[6] Since this road (as the Lord Himself says likewise) is so strait, and since there are so few that enter by it,[7] the soul considers it a great happiness and good chance to have passed along it to the said perfection of love, as it sings in this first stanza,[8] calling this strait road with full propriety 'dark night,' as will be explained hereafter in the lines of the said stanza. The soul, then, rejoicing at having passed along this narrow road whence so many blessings have come to it, speaks after this manner.

[6] Thus the Codices. E.p. and M read: 'along which the soul ordinarily passes in order to reach this high and Divine union with God.'
[7] St. Matthew vii, 14.
[8] Bz.: 'as it relates in this stanza.'

BOOK THE FIRST

Which treats of the Night of Sense.[1]

STANZA THE FIRST

**On a dark night, Kindled in love with yearnings—
oh, happy chance!—
I went forth without being observed, My house being
now at rest.**

EXPOSITION

In this first stanza the soul relates the way and manner which
it followed in going forth, as to its affection, from itself and
from all things, and in dying to them all and to itself, by
means of true mortification, in order to attain to living the
sweet and delectable life of love with God; and it says that
this going forth from itself and from all things was a 'dark
night,' by which, as will be explained hereafter, is here understood purgative contemplation, which causes passively[2] in the
soul the negation of itself and of all things referred to above.

2. And this going forth it says here that it was able to accomplish in the strength and ardour which love for its Spouse
gave to it for that purpose in the dark contemplation aforementioned. Herein it extols[3] the great happiness which it
found in journeying to God through this night with such
signal success that none of the three enemies, which are
world, devil and flesh (who are they that ever impede[4] this
road), could hinder it; inasmuch as the aforementioned night

---

[1] The Codices all begin with the stanza. The title belongs to the
e.p. only.

[2] E.p. omits 'passively.'

[3] V: 'desired to extol.'

[4] B, e.p.: 'disturb.'

of purgative[5] contemplation lulled to sleep and mortified, in the house of its sensuality, all the passions and desires with respect to their mischievous desires and motions.[6]

The line, then, says:

On a dark night

CHAPTER I

Sets down the first line and begins to treat of the imperfections of beginners.[1]

INTO this dark night souls begin to enter when God draws them forth from the state of beginners—which is the state of those that meditate on the spiritual road—and begins to set them in the state of progressives[2]—which is that of those who are already contemplatives—to the end that, after passing through it, they may arrive at the state of the perfect, which is that of the Divine union of the soul with God. Wherefore, to the end that we may the better understand and explain what night is this through which the soul passes, and for what cause God sets it therein, it will be well here to touch first of all upon certain characteristics of beginners (which, although we treat them with all possible brevity, will not fail to be of service likewise to the beginners themselves),[3] in order that, realizing the weakness of the state wherein they are, they may take courage, and may desire that God will bring them into this night, wherein the soul is strengthened and confirmed in the virtues, and made ready for the inestimable delights of the love of God. And, although we may tarry here for a time, it will not be for longer than is neces-

---

[5] [More exactly: 'purificative.'] E.p.: 'purified.'

[6] Thus B, C, G, H, M, Mtr. The other authorities and e.p. have: 'with respect to their mischievous motions.'

[1] From e.p.

[2] Thus [*aprovechantes*] A, B, C, E, G, H, Mtr. The other authorities, and e.p., read: '*aprovechados* ['proficient.']

[3] E.p. omits this parenthesis, which, however, is found in all the Codices, except C and E.

sary, so that we may go on to speak at once of this dark night.

2. It must be known, then, that the soul, after it has been definitely converted to the service of God, is, as a rule, spiritually nurtured and caressed by God, even as is the tender child by its loving mother, who warms it with the heat of her bosom and nurtures it with sweet milk and soft and pleasant food, and carries it and caresses it in her arms; but, as the child grows bigger, the mother gradually ceases caressing it, and, hiding her tender love, puts bitter aloes upon her sweet breast, sets down the child[4] from her arms and makes it walk upon its feet, so that it may lose the habits of a child and betake itself to more important and substantial occupations. The loving mother is like the grace of God, for, as soon as the soul is regenerated by its new warmth and fervour for the service of God, He treats it in the same way; He makes it to find spiritual milk, sweet and delectable, in all the things of God, without any labour of its own, and also great pleasure in spiritual exercises, for here God is giving to it the breast of His tender love, even as to a tender child.

3. Therefore, such a soul finds its delight in spending long periods—perchance whole nights—in prayer; penances are its pleasures; fasts its joys; and its consolations are to make use of the sacraments and to occupy itself in Divine things. In the which things spiritual persons (though taking part in them with great efficacy and persistence and using and treating them with great care) often find themselves, spiritually speaking, very weak and imperfect. For since they are moved to these things and to these spiritual exercises by the consolation and pleasure that they find in them, and since, too, they have not been prepared for them by the practice of earnest striving in the virtues, they have many faults and imperfections with respect to these spiritual actions of theirs; for, after all, any man's actions correspond to the habit of perfection attained by him. And, as these persons have not had the opportunity of acquiring the said habits of strength, they have necessarily to work like feeble[5] children, feebly. In order

---

[4] E.p. modifies these lines of the Codices, thus: 'and, hiding her tender breast, puts bitter aloes upon it, sets down the child.'

[5] E.p. and M omit 'feeble.'

that this may be seen more clearly, and likewise how much
these beginners in the virtues lack[6] with respect to the works
in which they so readily engage with the pleasure aforementioned, we shall describe it by reference to the seven capital
sins, each in its turn, indicating some of the many imperfections which they have under each heading; wherein it will be
clearly seen how like to children are these persons in all they
do. And it will also be seen how many blessings the dark
night of which we shall afterwards treat brings with it, since
it cleanses the soul and purifies it from all these imperfections.

CHAPTER II

*Of certain spiritual imperfections which beginners have with
respect to the habit of pride.*[1]

As these beginners feel themselves to be very fervent and
diligent in spiritual things and devout exercises, from this
prosperity[2] (although it is true that holy things of their own
nature cause humility) there often comes to them, through
their imperfections, a certain kind of secret pride, whence they
come to have some degree of satisfaction with their works
and with themselves. And hence there comes to them likewise
a certain desire, which is somewhat vain, and at times very
vain, to speak of spiritual things[3] in the presence of others, and
sometimes even to teach such things rather than to learn
them. They condemn others in their heart when they see
that they have not the kind of devotion which they themselves
desire; and sometimes they even say this in words, herein
resembling the Pharisee, who boasted of himself, praising God
for his own good works and despising the publican.[4]

---

[6] Thus B, G, H, Mtr., P, V. The other Codices and e.p. have:
'how feeble are these beginners in the virtues.'

[1] This title is found in e.p. and also in all the Codices.

[2] H, M: 'from this property.'

[3] E.p.: 'And hence there comes to them likewise a certain exceedingly vain desire to speak of spiritual things.'

[4] St. Luke xviii, 11–12.

2. In these persons the devil often increases the fervour that they have and the desire to perform these and other works more frequently, so that their pride and presumption may grow greater. For the devil knows quite well that all these works and virtues which they perform are not only value-less to them, but even become vices in them. And such a de-gree of evil are some of these persons wont to reach that they would have none appear good save themselves; and thus, in deed and word, whenever the opportunity occurs, they con-demn them and slander them, beholding the mote in their brother's eye[5] and not considering the beam which is in their own;[6] they strain at another's gnat and themselves swallow a camel.[7]

3. Sometimes, too, when their spiritual masters, such as confessors and superiors, do not approve of their spirit and behavior (for they are anxious that all they do shall be es-teemed and praised), they consider that they do not under-stand them, or that, because they do not approve of this and comply with that, their confessors are themselves not spiritual. And so they immediately desire and contrive to find some one else who will fit in with their tastes; for as a rule they de-sire to speak of spiritual matters with those who they think will praise and esteem what they do, and they flee, as they would from death, from those who disabuse them in order to lead them into a safe road—sometimes they even harbour ill-will against them. Presuming thus,[8] they are wont to re-solve much[9] and accomplish very little. Sometimes they are anxious that others shall realize how spiritual and devout they are, to which end they occasionally give outward evidence thereof in movements, sighs and other ceremonies; and at times they are apt to fall into[10] certain ecstasies, in public rather than in secret, wherein the devil aids them, and they

[5] E.p.: 'in another's eye.'
[6] St. Matthew vii, 3.
[7] St. Matthew xxiii, 24.
[8] [*Lit.*, 'Presuming.'] E.p. reads: 'Presuming upon themselves.'
[9] A, B abbreviate: '. . . who disabuse them in order to cause them fear. They are wont to resolve much.'
[10] The words 'they are apt to fall into' are found in e.p. alone.

are pleased that this should be noticed, and are often eager that it should be noticed more.[11]

4. Many such persons desire to be the favourites of their confessors and to become intimate with them[12], as a result of which there beset them continual occasions of envy and disquiet.[13] They are too much embarrassed[14] to confess their sins nakedly, lest their confessors should think less of them, so they palliate them and make them appear less evil, and thus it is to excuse themselves rather than to accuse themselves that they go to confession. And sometimes they seek another confessor to tell the wrongs that they have done, so that their own confessor shall think they have done nothing wrong at all, but only good; and thus they always take pleasure in telling him what is good,[15] and sometimes in such terms as make it appear to be greater than it is rather than less, desiring that he may think them to be good, when it would be greater humility in them, as we shall say, to depreciate it, and to desire that[16] neither he nor anyone else should consider them of account.

5. Some of these beginners, too, make little of their faults, and at other times become over-sad when they see themselves fall into them, thinking themselves to have been saints already; and thus they become angry and impatient with themselves, which is another imperfection. Often they beseech God, with great yearnings,[17] that He will take from them their imperfections and faults, but they do this that they may find themselves at peace, and may not be troubled by them, rather than for God's sake; not realizing that, if He should take their imperfections from them, they would probably become

[11] [The original merely has: 'and are often eager.'] E.p. modifies: 'that this about which they are so eager should be noticed.'

[12] E.p.: 'Many such desire to be intimate with their confessors.' H has: 'desire to preach [*predicar* for *preceder*] and to be intimate with their confessors,' which destroys the sense of the passage.

[13] [*Lit.,* 'a thousand envies and disquietudes.']

[14] Bz.: 'They are ashamed.'

[15] A, B, M omit: 'and thus . . . is good.'

[16] E.p.: 'and to say naught, so that . . .'

[17] M, e.p. omit 'great.'

prouder and more presumptuous[18] still. They dislike praising others and love to be praised themselves; sometimes they seek out such praise. Herein they are like the foolish virgins, who, when their lamps could not be lit, sought oil from others.[19]

6. From these imperfections some souls go on to develop[20] many very grave ones, which do them great harm. But some have fewer and some more,[21] and some, only the first motions thereof or little beyond these; and there are hardly any such beginners who, at the time of these signs of fervour,[22] fall not into some of these errors.[23] But those who at this time are going on to perfection proceed very differently and with quite another temper of spirit; for they progress by means of humility and are greatly edified, not only thinking naught of their own affairs,[24] but having very little satisfaction with themselves; they consider all others as far better, and usually have a holy envy of them, and an eagerness to serve God as they do. For the greater is their fervour, and the more numerous are the works that they perform, and the greater is the pleasure that they take in them, as they progress in humility, the more do they realize how much God deserves of them, and how little is all that they do for His sake;[25] and thus, the more they do, the less are they satisfied. So much would they gladly do from charity and love for Him, that all they do seems to them naught; and so greatly are they importuned, occupied and absorbed[26] by this loving anxiety that they never notice what others do or do not; or if they do notice it, they always believe, as I say, that all others are far better than they themselves. Wherefore, holding themselves as of little worth, they

[18] M, e.p. omit: 'and more presumptuous.'
[19] St. Matthew xxv, 8. [Lit., 'who, having their lamps dead, sought oil from without.']
[20] [Lit., 'to have.'] A, M omit this verb and read: 'go on to many . . .'
[21] E.p.: 'and others more.'
[22] [Lit., 'these fervours.']
[23] [Lit., 'into something of this.']
[24] E.p.: 'their own works.'
[25] H omits: 'and how . . . His sake.'
[26] Bz. has 'fascinated' for 'absorbed.' E.p.: 'importuned and occupied.'

are anxious that others too should thus hold them,[27] and should despise and depreciate that which they do. And further, if men should praise and esteem them, they can in no wise believe what they say; it seems to them strange that anyone should say these good things of them.

7. Together with great tranquillity and humbleness, these souls have a deep desire to be taught by anyone who can bring them profit; they are the complete opposite of those of whom we have spoken above, who would fain be always teaching, and who, when others seem to be teaching them, take the words from their mouths as if they knew them already. These souls, on the other hand, being far from desiring to be the masters of any, are very ready to travel and set out on another road than that which they are actually following, if they be so commanded, because they never think that they are right in anything whatsoever. They rejoice when others are praised; they grieve only because they serve not God like them. They have no desire to speak of the things that they do, because they think so little of them that they are ashamed to speak of them even to their spiritual masters, since they seem to them to be things that merit not being spoken of. They are more anxious to speak of their faults and sins, or that these should be recognized rather than their virtues;[28] and thus they incline to talk of their souls with those who account[29] their actions and their spirituality of little value. This is a characteristic of the spirit which is simple, pure, genuine and very pleasing to God. For as the wise Spirit of God dwells in these humble souls, He moves them and inclines them to keep His treasures secretly within and likewise to cast out from themselves all evil. God gives this grace to the humble, together with the other virtues, even as He denies it to the proud.

8. These souls will give their heart's blood to anyone that serves God, and will help others to serve Him as much as in them lies. The imperfections into which they see themselves

[27] A, B omit this clause [interrupting the sense of the passage].

[28] M, e.p.: 'or that it should be recognized that these [faults and sins] are not virtues.'

[29] E.p.: 'esteem.'

fall they bear with humility, meekness of spirit[30] and a loving fear of God, hoping in Him. But souls who in the beginning journey with this kind of perfection are, as I understand, and as has been said, a minority, and very few are those who we can be glad do not fall into the opposite errors. For this reason, as we shall afterwards say, God leads into the dark night those whom He desires to purify from all these imperfections so that He may bring them farther onward.

CHAPTER III

Of some imperfections which some of these souls[1] are apt to have, with respect to the second capital sin, which is avarice,[2] in the spiritual sense.

MANY of these beginners have also at times great spiritual avarice. They will be found to be discontented with the spirituality which God gives them; and they are very disconsolate and querulous because they find not in spiritual things the consolation that they would desire. Many can never have enough of listening to counsels and learning[3] spiritual precepts, and of possessing and reading many books which treat of this matter, and they spend their time on all these things rather than on works of mortification[4] and the perfecting[5] of the inward poverty of spirit which should be

[30] H: 'with humility, humility of spirit.'

[1] E.p.: 'which some beginners.'

[2] Bz.: 'which is pride and boasting.'

[3] M, e.p. omit 'learning.'

[4] Bz., P insert here: 'and they have and read many spiritual books which treat of this vice and of gluttony, which generally lead them to attempt many kinds of exercise, either to make great use of their capital, from a craving for great profits or through mere pleasure and cupidity; whence comes inconstancy to them and lack of stability in their particular exercises, which are chiefly necessary in these beginnings; and this spoils their labour and makes it of none effect and vain, wasting their time in experiments and trials.'

[5] E.p. reads: 'rather than on works, without the mortification and the perfecting.'

theirs. Furthermore, they burden themselves with images and
rosaries which are very curious;[6] now they put down one, now
take up another; now they change about, now change back
again; now they want this kind of thing, now that, preferring
one kind of cross to another, because it is more curious.[7]
And others you will see adorned with agnusdeis[8] and relics
and tokens,[9] like children with trinkets. Here I condemn the
attachment of the heart, and the affection which they have
for the nature, multitude and curiosity of these things, inasmuch as it is quite contrary to poverty of spirit, which considers
only the substance of devotion, makes use only of what
suffices for that end and grows weary of this other kind of
multiplicity and curiosity. For true devotion must issue from
the heart, and consist in the truth and substance[10] alone of
what is represented by spiritual things; all the rest is affection
and attachment proceeding from imperfection; and in order
that one may pass to any kind of perfection[11] it is necessary
for such desires to be killed.

2. I knew a person who for more than ten years made use
of a cross roughly formed from a branch[12] that had been
blessed, fastened with a pin twisted round it; he had never
ceased using it, and he always carried it about with him
until I took it from him; and this was a person of no small

---

[6] So H, P. A, B, C, G, Mtr., V have: 'which are sometimes very
curious and showy.' So Bz., but with 'costly' for 'showy.' M, e.p.:
'images and crosses which are very curious and costly.'

[7] Bz. adds: 'or costly.' Other authorities add: 'or valuable.'

[8] The *agnusdei* was a wax medal with a representation of the lamb
stamped upon it, often blessed by the Pope; at the time of the Saint
such medals were greatly sought after, as we know from various
references in St. Teresa's letters.

[9] [The word *nómina*, translated 'token,' and normally meaning
'list' or 'roll,' refers to a relic on which were written the names of
saints. In modern Spanish it can denote a medal or amulet used
superstitiously.]

[10] E.p. alone modifies thus: 'from the heart, in truth alone, and
must consider only the truth and substance.'

[11] E.p. alone has: 'pass to the estate of perfection.'

[12] [No doubt a branch of palm, olive or rosemary, blessed in church
on Palm Sunday, like the English palm crosses of to-day. 'Palm Sunday' is in Spanish *Domingo de ramos*: 'Branch Sunday.']

sense and understanding. And I saw another who said his
prayers using beads that were made of bones from the spine
of a fish; his devotion was certainly no less precious on that
account in the sight of God, for it is clear that these things[13]
carried no devotion in their workmanship or value. Those,
then, who start from these beginnings and make good progress attach themselves to no visible instruments, nor do they
burden themselves with such, nor desire to know more than
is necessary in order that they may act well;[14] for they set
their eyes only on being right with God and on pleasing Him,
and therein consists their covetousness. And thus with great
generosity they give away all that they have, and delight
to know that they have it not, for God's sake and for charity
to their neighbour,[15] no matter whether these be spiritual
things or temporal. For, as I say, they set their eyes only
upon the reality of interior[16] perfection, which is to give
pleasure to God and in naught to give pleasure to themselves.

3. But neither from these imperfections nor from those
others can the soul be perfectly purified until God brings
it into the passive purgation of that dark night whereof we
shall speak presently. It befits the soul, however, to contrive to
labour, in so far as it can, on its own account, to the end
that it may purge and perfect itself, and thus may merit being
taken by God into that Divine care wherein it becomes
healed of all things that it was unable of itself to cure. Because, however greatly the soul itself labours, it cannot[17]
actively purify itself so as to be in the least degree prepared
for the Divine union of perfection of love, if God takes not[18]
its hand and purges it not in that dark fire, in the way and
manner that we have to describe.[19]

[13] Thus e.p. alone. The other authorities have 'these.'
[14] M: 'neither do they desire to know much in order to act [well].'
[The word 'well' does not occur anywhere in the original.]
[15] E.p.: 'and for charity to their neighbour, ruling everything by
the laws of this virtue.'
[16] M, e.p. omit 'interior.'
[17] E.p.: 'it cannot by its industry.'
[18] M, e.p.: 'of love with God, if He takes not.'
[19] E.p.: 'in the manner that we have to describe'; M: 'in the manner that we have described.'

CHAPTER IV

Of other imperfections which these beginners are apt to have with respect to the third sin, which is luxury.[1]

MANY of these beginners have many other imperfections than those which I am describing with respect to each of the deadly sins, but these I set aside, in order to avoid prolixity, touching upon a few of the most important, which are, as it were, the origin and cause[2] of the rest. And thus, with respect to this sin of luxury (leaving apart the falling of spiritual persons[3] into this sin, since my intent is to treat of the imperfections which have to be purged by the dark night), they have many imperfections which[4] might be described as spiritual luxury, not because they are so, but because the imperfections proceed from spiritual things. For it often comes to pass that, in their very spiritual exercises, when they are powerless to prevent it, there arise and assert themselves in the sensual part of the soul impure acts and motions,[5] and sometimes this happens even when the spirit is deep in prayer, or engaged in the Sacrament of Penance or in the Eucharist. These things are not, as I say, in their power; they proceed from one of three causes.[6]

2. The first cause from which they often proceed is the

[1] E.p. adds: 'spiritually understood.'

[2] Bz.: 'origin and head.'

[3] E.p. omits: 'of spiritual persons.' [This is a better reading: the omission throws into relief the author's contrast between the actual commission of the deadly sin and the imperfections connected with it.]

[4] So e.p. The Codices read [more emphatically]: 'many imperfections, many which.'

[5] E.p.: 'in the sensual part of the soul unclean motions.' The edition of 1630 reads: 'not because this is so, but because at times it is felt and experienced in the flesh, by reason of its weakness, when the soul receives spiritual things. For it often comes to pass that, in their very spiritual exercises, when they are powerless to prevent it, there arise and are experienced in the sensual part of the soul unclean motions.'

[6] Thus most of the Codices. Others, and e.p., read: 'three things.'

pleasure which human nature takes in spiritual things.[7] For when the spirit and the sense are pleased, every part of a man is moved by that pleasure[8] to delight according to its proportion[9] and nature. For then the spirit, which is the higher part, is moved to pleasure[10] and delight in God; and the sensual nature, which is the lower part, is moved to pleasure and delight of the senses, because it cannot possess and lay hold upon aught else, and it therefore lays hold upon that which comes nearest to itself, which is the impure and sensual.[11] Thus it comes to pass that the soul is in deep prayer with God according to the spirit, and, on the other hand, according to sense it is passively conscious, not without great displeasure, of rebellions and motions and acts of the senses,[12] which often happens in Communion, for when the soul receives joy and comfort in this act of love, because this Lord bestows it (since it is to that end that He gives Himself), the sensual nature takes that which is its own likewise, as we have said, after its manner. Now as, after all, these two parts are combined in one individual, they ordinarily both participate in that which one of them receives, each after its manner; for, as the philosopher says, everything that is received is in the recipient[13] after the manner of the same recipient. And thus, in these beginnings, and even when the soul has made some progress, its sensual part, being imperfect, oftentimes receives the Spirit of God with the same imperfection.[14] Now when this sensual part is renewed by the purgation of the dark night

[7] E.p.: '. . . occasionally proceed, albeit rarely and in weak natures, is from,' etc.

[8] [Lit., 'recreation.']

[9] So H, P. The other authorities [followed by P. Silverio] have 'portion.'

[10] [Lit., 'recreation.']

[11] E.p. omits: 'and it . . . and sensual.'

[12] E.p. reads: 'Thus it comes to pass that the soul is in prayer with God according to the spirit, and, on the other hand, according to sense it is passively conscious, not without great displeasure, of rebellions and motions of the senses.' It then omits the following words: 'which often . . . after its manner.'

[13] E.p. omits: 'in the recipient.'

[14] E.p.: 'since its sensual part is imperfect, it occasionally partakes of spiritual pleasures with the same imperfection.'

which we shall describe, it no longer has these weaknesses; for it is no longer this part that receives aught, but rather it is itself received into the Spirit. And thus it then has everything after the manner of the Spirit.[15]

3. The second cause whence these rebellions sometimes proceed is the devil, who, in order to disquiet[16] and disturb the soul, at times when it is at prayer or is striving to pray, contrives to stir up these motions of impurity in its nature; and if the soul gives heed to any of these, they cause it great harm. For through fear of these not only do persons become lax in prayer—which is the aim of the devil when he begins to strive with them—but some give up prayer altogether, because they think that these things attack them more during that exercise than apart from it, which is true, since the devil attacks them then more than at other times, so that they may give up spiritual exercises. And not only so, but he succeeds in portraying to them very vividly things that are most foul and impure, and at times are very closely related to certain spiritual things and persons that are of profit to their souls, in order to terrify them and make them fearful;[17] so that those who are affected by this dare not even look at anything or meditate upon anything, because they immediately encounter this temptation. And upon those who are inclined to melancholy this acts with such effect[18] that they become greatly to be pitied since they are suffering so sadly; for this trial reaches such a point in certain persons, when they have this evil humour, that they believe it to be clear that the devil is ever present with them and that they have no power to prevent this, although some of these persons can prevent his attack

[15] E.p. expands thus: '. . . has these weaknesses; for so abundantly does it receive the Divine Spirit that it seems rather to be received into that same Spirit—into One, in brief, that is very much greater. And thus it possesses everything after the manner of the Spirit, in a wondrous way, in Whom it is a partaker, being united with God.'

[16] M, V: 'to disgust'; Mtr.: 'to retaliate.'

[17] E.p. has 'make an end of them' [acabarlas] for 'make them fearful' [acobardarlas].

[18] So H. A, B, Bz., G, Mtr., P, V have: 'with such effect and frequency.' M, e.p.: 'with such effect and vehemence.'

by dint of great effort and labour.[19] When these impurities[20] attack such souls through the medium of melancholy, they are not as a rule freed from them until they have been cured of that kind of humour, unless the dark night has entered the soul, and rids them of all impurities, one after another.[21]

4. The third source whence these impure motions are apt to proceed in order to make war upon the soul is often the fear which such persons have conceived for these impure representations and motions. Something that they see or say or think brings them to their mind, and this makes them afraid, so that they suffer from them through no fault of their own.

5.[22] There are also certain souls of so tender and frail a nature that, when there comes to them some spiritual consolation or some grace in prayer, the spirit of luxury is with them immediately, inebriating[23] and delighting their sensual nature in such manner that it is as if they were plunged into the enjoyment and pleasure of this sin; and the enjoyment remains, together with the consolation, passively, and sometimes they are able to see that certain impure and unruly acts have taken place. The reason for this is that, since these natures are, as I say, frail and tender, their humours are stirred up and their blood is excited at the least disturbance.[24] And hence come these motions; and the same thing happens to such souls when they are enkindled with anger or suffer any disturbance or grief.[25]

---

[19] E.p. omits: 'since they are suffering . . . effort and labour.' C also omits these lines and a number of other passages in this chapter.

[20] E.p.: 'these things.'

[21] [*Lit.*, 'of everything.'] E.p.: 'and gradually purifies them altogether.'

[22] C omits most of this paragraph and e.p. omits it all.

[23] M has 'hindering' [*embarga*] for 'inebriating' [*embriaga*].

[24] V: 'the least operation.'

[25] All writers who comment upon this delicate matter go into lengthy and learned explanations of it, though in reality there is little that needs to be added to the Saint's clear and apt exposition. It will be remembered that St. Teresa once wrote to her brother Lorenzo, who suffered in this way: 'As to those stirrings of sense. . . . I am quite clear they are of no account, so the best thing is to

6. Sometimes, again, there arises within these spiritual persons, whether they be speaking or performing spiritual actions, a certain vigour and bravado, through their having regard to persons who are present, and before these persons they display a certain kind of vain gratification. This also arises from luxury of spirit, after the manner wherein we here understand it, which is accompanied as a rule[26] by complacency in the will.

7.[27] Some of these persons make friendships of a spiritual kind with others, which oftentimes arise from luxury and not from spirituality; this may be known to be the case when the remembrance of that friendship causes not the remembrance and love of God to grow, but occasions remorse of conscience. For, when the friendship is purely spiritual, the love of God grows with it; and the more the soul remembers it, the more it remembers the love of God, and the greater the desire it has for God; so that, as the one grows, the other grows also. For the spirit of God has this property, that it increases good by adding to it more good, inasmuch as there is likeness and conformity between them. But, when this love arises from the vice of sensuality aforementioned, it produces the contrary effects; for the more the one grows, the more the other decreases, and the remembrance of it likewise. If that sensual love grows, it will at once be observed that the soul's love of God is becoming colder, and that it is forgetting Him as it remembers that love; there comes to it, too, a certain remorse of conscience. And, on the other hand, if the love of God grows in the soul, that other love becomes cold and is forgotten; for, as the two are contrary to one another, not only does the one not aid the other, but the one which predominates quenches and confounds the other, and becomes strengthened in itself, as the philosophers say. Wherefore

---

make no account of them' (LL. 168). The most effective means of calming souls tormented by these favours is to commend them to a discreet and wise director whose counsel they may safely follow. The Illuminists committed the grossest errors in dealing with this matter.

[26] E.p. reads 'at times' for 'as a rule.'

[27] H, V insert here a sub-title: 'Rule for knowing the love which is with God and that which is not so.'

Our Saviour said in the Gospel: 'That which is born of the flesh is flesh, and that which is born of the Spirit is spirit.'[28] That is to say, the love which is born of sensuality ends in sensuality, and that which is of the spirit ends in the spirit of God and causes it to grow. This is the difference that exists between these two kinds of love, whereby we may know them.

8. When the soul enters the dark night, it brings these kinds of love under control. It strengthens and purifies the one, namely that which is according to God; and the other it removes and brings to an end;[29] and in the beginning it causes both to be lost sight of, as we shall say hereafter.

CHAPTER V

Of the imperfections into which beginners fall with respect to the sin of wrath.

By reason of the concupiscence which many beginners have for spiritual consolations, their experience of these consolations is very commonly accompanied by many imperfections proceeding from the sin of wrath; for, when their delight and pleasure in spiritual things come to an end, they naturally become embittered,[1] and bear that lack of sweetness which they have to suffer with a bad grace, which affects all that they do; and they very easily become irritated over the smallest matter—sometimes, indeed, none can tolerate them. This frequently happens after they have been very pleasantly recollected in prayer according to sense; when their pleasure and delight therein come to an end, their nature is naturally vexed and disappointed, just as is the child when they take it from the breast of which it was enjoying the sweetness. There is no sin in this natural vexation,[2] when it is not permitted

---

[28] St. John iii, 6.
[29] E.p.: 'removes, brings to an end or mortifies.'
[1] *desabridos.*
[2] M: 'natural disillusion.'

to indulge itself, but only imperfection, which must be purged by the aridity and severity of the dark night.

2. There are other of these spiritual persons, again, who fall into another kind of spiritual wrath: this happens when they become irritated at the sins of others, and keep watch on those others with a sort of uneasy zeal. At times the impulse comes to them to reprove them angrily, and occasionally they go so far as to indulge it[3] and set themselves up as masters of virtue. All this is contrary to spiritual meekness.

3. There are others who are vexed with themselves when they observe their own imperfectness,[4] and display an impatience that is not humility; so impatient are they about this that they would fain be saints in a day. Many of these persons purpose to accomplish a great deal and make grand[5] resolutions; yet, as they are not humble and have no misgivings about themselves,[6] the more resolutions they make, the greater is their fall and the greater their annoyance, since they have not the patience to wait for that which God will give them when it pleases Him; this likewise is contrary to the spiritual meekness[7] aforementioned, which cannot be wholly remedied save by the purgation of the dark night. Some souls, on the other hand, are so patient[8] as regards the progress which they desire that God would gladly see them less so.

CHAPTER VI

Of imperfections with respect to spiritual gluttony.

WITH respect to the fourth sin, which is spiritual gluttony, there is much to be said, for there is scarce one of these

[3] [*Lit.*, 'they even do it.'] E.p.: 'they even carry it out.'

[4] M: 'impatience' for 'imperfectness.'

[5] Some Codices read: 'make many.'

[6] So A, G, H, M, Mtr. The other authorities read: 'nor trust in themselves' [*confían* for *desconfían*].

[7] All the MSS. have 'meekness.' H reads 'dishonour,' which a corrector has altered to 'misgivings' [*desconfianza*].

[8] E.p. adds: 'and travel so slowly.'

beginners who, however satisfactory his progress, falls not into some of the many imperfections which come to these beginners with respect to this sin, on account of the sweetness which they find at first in spiritual exercises. For many of these, lured by the sweetness and pleasure which they find in such exercises, strive more after spiritual sweetness than after spiritual purity and discretion,[1] which is that which God regards and accepts throughout the spiritual journey.[2] Therefore, besides the imperfections into which the seeking for sweetness of this kind makes them fall, the gluttony which they now have makes them continually go to extremes, so that they pass beyond the limits of moderation within which the virtues are acquired and wherein they have their being. For some of these persons, attracted by the pleasure which they find therein, kill themselves with penances, and others weaken themselves with fasts, by performing more than their frailty can bear, without the order or advice of any,[3] but rather endeavouring to avoid those whom they should obey in these matters; some, indeed, dare to do these things even though the contrary has been commanded them.

2. These persons are most imperfect and unreasonable; for they set bodily penance before subjection and obedience, which is penance according to reason and discretion, and therefore a sacrifice more acceptable and pleasing to God than any other. But such one-sided penance is no more than the penance of beasts, to which they are attracted, exactly like beasts, by the desire and pleasure which they find therein.[4] Inasmuch as all extremes are vicious, and as in behaving thus such persons[5] are working their own will, they grow in vice rather than in virtue; for, to say the least, they are acquiring spiritual gluttony and pride in this way, through not

[1] E.p.: 'than after true devotion and purity.'

[2] [Lit., 'spiritual road.']

[3] A, P: 'without any order or advice.' H: 'without order and advice.'

[4] E.p. softens thus: 'Such one-sided penance is most imperfect, for they are attracted thereto only by the desire and pleasure which they find therein.'

[5] [Lit., 'these persons.' M, e.p.: 'all persons.']

walking in obedience. And many of these the devil assails,[6] stirring up this gluttony in them through the pleasures and desires which he increases within them, to such an extent that, since they can no longer help themselves, they either change or vary or add to that which is commanded them, as any obedience in this respect is so bitter[7] to them. To such an evil pass have some persons come that, simply because it is through obedience that they engage in these exercises, they lose the desire and devotion to perform them, their only desire and pleasure being to do what they themselves are inclined to do,[8] so that it would probably be more profitable for them not to engage in these exercises at all.

3. You will find that many of these persons are very insistent with their spiritual masters to be granted that which they desire, extracting it from them almost by force; if they be refused it they become as peevish as children and go about in great displeasure, thinking that they are not serving God when they are not allowed to do that which they would. For they go about clinging to their own will and pleasure, which they treat as though it came from God;[9] and immediately their directors[10] take it from them, and try to subject them to the will of God, they become peevish, grow faint-hearted and fall away. These persons think that their own satisfaction and pleasure are the satisfaction and service of God.

4. There are others, again, who, because of this gluttony, know so little of their own unworthiness and misery and have thrust so far from them the loving fear and reverence which they owe to the greatness of God, that they hesitate not to insist continually that their confessors shall allow them to communicate[11] often. And, what is worse, they frequently dare to communicate without the leave and consent[12] of

[6] E.p.: 'the devil deceives.'

[7] E.p.: 'so severe and bitter.'

[8] C, G, Mtr., V add: 'and not because it is commanded them.'

[9] [Lit., 'and treat this as their God.'] This e.p. omits [softening the sense of the whole, as above (p. 54)].

[10] The Spanish is impersonal: 'immediately this is taken from them,' etc.]

[11] G, M, e.p.: 'to confess and communicate.'

[12] [Lit., 'and opinion.']

the minister and steward of Christ, merely acting on their own opinion, and contriving to conceal the truth from him. And for this reason, because they desire to communicate continually, they make their confessions[13] carelessly,[14] being more eager to eat than to eat cleanly and perfectly, although it would be healthier and holier for them had they the contrary inclination and begged their confessors not to command them to approach the altar so frequently: between these two extremes, however, the better way is that of humble resignation. But the boldness referred to is[15] a thing that does great harm, and men may fear to be punished for such temerity.

5. These persons, in communicating, strive with every nerve to obtain some kind of sensible sweetness and pleasure, instead of humbly doing reverence and giving praise within themselves to God. And in such wise do they devote themselves to this that, when they have received no pleasure or sweetness in the senses, they think that they have accomplished nothing at all. This is to judge God very unworthily; they have not realized that the least of the benefits which come from this Most Holy Sacrament is that which concerns the senses; and that the invisible part of the grace that it bestows is much greater; for, in order that they may look at it with the eyes of faith, God oftentimes withholds from them these other consolations and sweetnesses of sense.[16] And thus they desire to feel and taste God as though He were comprehensible by them and accessible to them, not only in this, but likewise in other spiritual practices. All this is very great imperfection and completely opposed to the nature of God, since it is impurity in faith.[17]

6. These persons have the same defect as regards the practice of prayer, for they think that all the business of prayer consists in experiencing sensible pleasure and devotion and

[13] H erroneously reads: 'their passions.'

[14] [Lit., 'anyhow.']

[15] [Lit., 'the other boldnesses are.'] A, e.p. read: 'the excessive boldnesses are.'

[16] M, e.p.: 'and favours of sense.' [The difference, in a Spanish MS., between sabores and favores would be of the slightest.]

[17] So the MSS. E.p. modifies the last clause and reads: 'Who demands the purest faith.'

they strive to obtain this by great effort,[18] wearying and
fatiguing their faculties and their heads; and when they have
not found this pleasure they become greatly discouraged,
thinking that they have accomplished nothing. Through
these efforts they lose true devotion and spirituality, which
consist in perseverance, together with patience and humility,
and mistrust of themselves, that they may please God alone.
For this reason, when they have once failed to find pleasure
in this or some other exercise, they have great disinclination
and repugnance to return to it, and at times they abandon it.
They are, in fact, as we have said, like children, who are not
influenced by reason, and who act, not from rational motives,
but from inclination.[19] Such persons expend all their effort
in seeking spiritual pleasure and consolation; they never tire,
therefore, of reading books; and they begin, now one meditation, now another, in their pursuit of this pleasure which
they desire to experience in the things of God. But God, very
justly, wisely and lovingly, denies it to them, for otherwise this
spiritual gluttony and inordinate appetite would breed innumerable evils. It is, therefore, very fitting that they should
enter into the dark night, whereof we shall speak,[20] that they
may be purged from this childishness.

7. These persons who are thus inclined to such pleasures
have another very great imperfection, which is that they are
very weak and remiss in journeying upon the hard[21] road of
the Cross; for the soul that is given to sweetness naturally has
its face set against all self-denial, which is devoid of sweetness.[22]

8. These persons have many other imperfections which
arise hence, of which in time the Lord heals them by means
of temptations, aridities and other trials, all of which are

[18] [*Lit.*, 'they strive to obtain this, as they say, by the strength of
their arms.' The phrase is, of course, understood in the Spanish to
be metaphorical, as the words 'as they say' clearly indicate.]
[19] [*Lit.*, 'who are not influenced, neither act by reason, but from
pleasure.']
[20] [*Lit.*, 'which we shall give.'] E.p. omits: 'whereof we shall
speak.' A, G, V: 'which we shall describe.'
[21] [*áspero*: harsh, rough, rugged.]
[22] [*Lit.*, 'against all the sweetlessness of self-denial.']

part of the dark night. All these I will not treat further here, lest I become too lengthy; I will only say that spiritual temperance and sobriety lead to another and a very different temper, which is that of mortification, fear and submission in all things. It thus becomes clear that the perfection and worth of things consist not in the multitude and the pleasantness of one's actions,[23] but in being able to deny oneself in them; this such persons must endeavour to compass, in so far as they may, until God is pleased to purify them indeed, by bringing them[24] into the dark night, to arrive at which I am hastening on with my account of these imperfections.

CHAPTER VII

Of imperfections with respect to spiritual envy and sloth.[1]

WITH respect likewise to the other two vices, which are spiritual envy and sloth, these beginners fail not to have many imperfections. For, with respect to envy, many of them are wont to experience movements[2] of displeasure at the spiritual good of others, which cause them a certain sensible grief at being outstripped upon this road, so that they would prefer not to hear others praised; for they become displeased at others' virtues and sometimes they cannot refrain from contradicting what is said in praise of them, depreciating it as far as they can; and their annoyance thereat grows[3] because the same[4] is not said of them, for they would fain be preferred in everything. All this is clean contrary to charity,

---

[23] Bz., M: 'of one's things.' E.p. abbreviates: 'in the multitude of one's actions.'

[24] [*Lit.*, 'causing them to enter.'] Bz.: 'putting them.'

[1] Bz., H omit: 'and sloth.'

[2] Bz. qualifies with 'many.'

[3] [*Lit.*, 'and, as they say, their eye (*el ojo*) grows'—a colloquial phrase expressing annoyance.] E.p. omits this phrase altogether. Bz., G read *enojo* for *el ojo* [destroying the metaphor but not altering the sense of this translation.]

[4] E.p.: 'and they greatly regret that the same.'

which, as Saint Paul says, rejoices in goodness.[5] And, if charity
has any envy, it is a holy envy, comprising grief at not having
the virtues of others, yet also joy because others have them,
and delight when others outstrip us in the service of God,
wherein we ourselves are so remiss.

2. With respect also to spiritual sloth, beginners are apt to
be irked by the things that are most spiritual, from which
they flee because these things are incompatible with sensible
pleasure. For, as they are so much accustomed to sweetness in
spiritual things, they are wearied by things in which they find
no sweetness. If once they failed to find in prayer the satisfaction which their taste required (and after all it is well that
God should take it from them to prove them), they would
prefer not to return to it: sometimes they leave it; at other
times they continue it unwillingly. And thus because of this
sloth they abandon the way of perfection (which is the way of
the negation of their will and pleasure for God's sake) for the
pleasure and sweetness of their own will, which they aim at
satisfying in this way rather than the will of God.

3. And many of these would have God will that which they
themselves will, and are fretful at having to will that which
He wills, and find it repugnant to accommodate their will
to that of God.[6] Hence it happens to them that oftentimes
they think that that wherein they find not their own will and
pleasure is not the will of God; and that, on the other hand,
when they themselves find satisfaction, God is satisfied. Thus
they measure God by themselves and not themselves by God,
acting quite contrarily to that which He Himself taught in
the Gospel, saying: That he who should lose his will for His
sake, the same should gain it; and he who should desire to gain
it, the same should lose it.[7]

4. These persons likewise find it irksome when they are
commanded to do that wherein they take no pleasure. Because they aim at spiritual sweetness and consolation, they

[5] 1 Corinthians xiii, 6. The Saint here cites the sense, not the
letter, of the epistle. B, H give the quotation correctly, as 'rejoiceth
in the truth.'

[6] E.p.: 'to the Divine will.'

[7] St. Matthew xvi, 25.

are too weak to have the fortitude and bear the trials of perfection.[8] They resemble those who are softly nurtured and who run fretfully away from everything that is hard, and take offence at the Cross, wherein consist the delights of the spirit. The more spiritual a thing is, the more irksome they find it, for, as they seek to go about spiritual matters with complete freedom and according to the inclination of their will, it causes them great sorrow and repugnance to enter upon the narrow way, which, says Christ, is the way of life.[9]

5. Let it suffice here to have described these imperfections, among the many to be found in the lives of those that are in this first state of beginners, so that it may be seen how greatly they need God to set them in the state of proficients. This He does by bringing them into the dark night whereof we now speak; wherein He weans them from the breasts of these sweetnesses and pleasures, gives them pure aridities and inward darkness, takes from them all these irrelevances[10] and puerilities, and by very different means causes them to win the virtues. For, however assiduously the beginner practises the mortification in himself of all these actions and passions of his, he can never completely succeed—very far from it—until God shall work it in him passively by means of the purgation of the said night. Of this I would fain speak in some way that may be profitable; may God, then, be pleased to give me His Divine light, because this is very needful in a night that is so dark and a matter that is so difficult[11] to describe and to expound.

The line, then, is:

In a dark night.

---

[8] [*Lit.*, 'they are very weak for the fortitude and trial of perfection.']

[9] St. Matthew vii, 14.

[10] M, P, e.p.: 'all these imperfections.'

[11] E.p. and a number of MSS. omit all that follows the word 'difficult.'

CHAPTER VIII

Wherein is expounded the first line of the first stanza, and a beginning is made of the explanation of this dark night.[1]

THIS night, which, as we say, is contemplation, produces in spiritual persons two kinds of darkness or purgation, corresponding to the two parts of man's nature—namely, the sensual and the spiritual. And thus the one night or purgation will be sensual, wherein the soul is purged according to sense, which is subdued to the spirit; and the other is a night or purgation which is spiritual, wherein the soul is purged and stripped[2] according to the spirit, and subdued and made ready for the union of love with God. The night of sense is common and comes to many: these are the beginners; and of this night[3] we shall speak first. The night of the spirit is the portion of very few, and these are they that are already practised and proficient, of whom we shall treat hereafter.

2. The first purgation or night is bitter and terrible to sense, as we shall now show.[4] The second bears no comparison with it, for it is horrible and awful[5] to the spirit, as we shall show[6] presently. Since the night of sense is first in order and comes first, we shall first of all[7] say something about it briefly, since more is written of it, as of a thing that is more common; and we shall pass on to treat more fully of the spiritual night, since very little has been said of this, either in speech[8] or in writing, and very little[9] is known of it, even by experience.

3. Since, then, the conduct of these beginners upon the way

---

[1] The title is taken from e.p. The Codices have no title.
[2] E.p.: 'wherein a soul is purged or stripped.'
[3] E.p.: 'of whom.'
[4] [*Lit.,* 'say.']
[5] E.p.: 'for it is very awful.'
[6] [*Lit.,* 'say.']
[7] E.p. omits: 'first of all.'
[8] [*plática*: the word is frequently used in Spanish to denote an informal sermon or address.]
[9] This 'very little' [which in the original comes in the emphatic final position] is omitted in e.p.

of God is ignoble,[10] and has much to do with their love of self and their own inclinations, as has been explained above, God desires to lead them farther. He seeks to bring them out of that ignoble kind of love to a higher degree of love for Him, to free them from the ignoble exercises of sense and meditation (wherewith, as we have said, they go seeking God so unworthily and in so many ways that are unbefitting), and to lead them to a kind of spiritual exercise wherein they can commune with Him more abundantly and are freed more completely from imperfections. For they have now had practice for some time in the way of virtue and have persevered in meditation and prayer, whereby, through the sweetness and pleasure that they have found therein, they have lost their love of the things of the world and have gained some degree of spiritual strength in God; this has enabled them to some extent to refrain from creature desires, so that for God's sake they are now able to suffer a light burden and a little aridity without turning back to a time[11] which they found more pleasant. When they are going about these spiritual exercises with the greatest delight and pleasure, and when they believe that the sun of Divine favour is shining most brightly upon them, God turns all this light of theirs into darkness, and shuts against them the door and the source of the sweet spiritual water which they were tasting in God whensoever and for as long as they desired. (For, as they were weak and tender, there was no door closed to them, as Saint John says in the Apocalypse, iii, 8). And thus He leaves them so completely in the dark that they know not whither to go with their sensible imagination and meditation; for they cannot[12] advance a step in meditation, as they were wont to do aforetime, their inward senses being submerged in this night, and left with such dryness that not only do they experience no pleasure and consolation in the spiritual things and good exercises wherein they were wont to find their delights and pleasures, but instead, on the contrary, they find insipidity and

[10] [*Lit.*, 'low'; the same word recurs below and is similarly translated.]

[11] [*Lit.*, 'to the better time.']

[12] M, e.p.: 'for they know not how to.'

bitterness in the said things. For, as I have said, God now sees that they have grown a little, and are becoming strong enough to lay aside their swaddling clothes and be taken from the gentle breast; so He sets them down from His arms and teaches them to[13] walk on their own feet; which they feel to be very strange, for everything seems to be going wrong with them.

4. To recollected persons this commonly happens sooner after their beginnings than to others, inasmuch as they are freer from occasions of backsliding, and their desires turn more quickly from the things of the world, which is necessary if they are to begin to enter this blessed[14] night of sense. Ordinarily no great time passes after their beginnings before they begin to enter this night of sense; and the great majority of them do in fact enter it, for they will generally be seen to fall into these aridities.

5. With regard to this way of purgation of the senses, since it is so common, we might here adduce a great number of quotations from Divine Scripture, where many passages relating to it are continually found, particularly in the Psalms and the Prophets. However, I do not wish to spend time upon these, for he who knows not how to look for them there will find the common experience of this purgation to be sufficient.[15]

CHAPTER IX

Of the signs by which it will be known that the spiritual person is walking along the way of this night and purgation of sense.

BUT since these aridities might frequently proceed, not from the night and purgation of the sensual desires aforementioned,

---

[13] M, e.p.: 'and shows them how to.'
[14] E.p. has 'happy' for 'blessed.'
[15] C, e.p. omit this entire sentence, substituting: 'And, to avoid prolixity, we omit them, albeit we shall adduce certain of them later.'

but from sins and imperfections, or from weakness and luke-warmness, or from some bad humour or indisposition of the body, I shall here set down certain signs by which it may be known if such aridity proceeds from the aforementioned purgation, or if it arises from any of the aforementioned sins. For the making of this distinction I find that there are three principal signs.

2. The first is whether, when a soul finds no pleasure or consolation in the things of God, it also fails to find it in any thing created; for, as God sets the soul in this dark night to the end that He may quench and purge its sensual desire, He allows it not to find attraction or sweetness in anything whatsoever. In such a case it may be considered very probable[1] that this aridity and insipidity proceed not from recently committed sins or imperfections. For, if this were so, the soul would feel in its nature some inclination or desire to taste other things than those of God; since, whenever the desire is allowed indulgence in any imperfection, it immediately feels inclined thereto, whether little or much, in proportion to the pleasure and the love that it has put into it. Since, however, this lack of enjoyment in things above or below might proceed from some indisposition or melancholy humour, which oftentimes makes it impossible for the soul to take pleasure in anything, it becomes necessary to apply the second sign and condition.

3. The second sign whereby a man may believe himself to be experiencing the said purgation[2] is that the memory is ordinarily centred upon God, with painful care and solicitude, thinking that it is not serving God, but is backsliding, because it finds itself without sweetness in the things of God. And in such a case it is evident that this lack of sweetness and this aridity come not from weakness and lukewarmness; for it is the nature of lukewarmness not to care greatly or to have any inward solicitude for the things of God. There is thus a great difference between aridity and lukewarmness, for lukewarmness consists in great weakness and remissness in the will and in the spirit, without solicitude as to serving God;

[1] [Lit., 'And in this it is known very probably.'] E.p. omits 'very.'
[2] E.p.: 'The second sign and condition of this purgation.'

whereas purgative aridity is ordinarily accompanied by solicitude, with care and grief as I say, because the soul is not
serving God. And, although this may sometimes be increased
by melancholy or some other humour (as it frequently is), it
fails not for that reason to produce a purgative effect upon
the desire, since the desire is deprived of all pleasure,[3] and has
its care centred upon God alone. For, when mere humour is
the cause, it spends itself in displeasure and ruin of the
physical nature, and there are none of those desires to serve
God which belong to purgative aridity. When the cause is
aridity, it is true that the sensual part of the soul has fallen
low, and is weak and feeble in its actions, by reason of the
little pleasure which it finds in them; but the spirit, on the
other hand, is ready and strong.

4. For the cause of this aridity is that God transfers to the
spirit the good things and the strength of the senses, which,
since the soul's natural strength and senses are incapable of
using them, remain barren, dry and empty. For the sensual
part of a man has no capacity for that which is pure spirit,
and thus, when it is the spirit that receives the pleasure, the
flesh is left without savour and is too weak to perform any
action. But the spirit, which all the time is being fed, goes
forward in strength, and with more alertness and solicitude
than before, in its anxiety not to fail God; and if it is not
immediately conscious of spiritual sweetness and delight, but
only of aridity and lack of sweetness, the reason for this is the
strangeness of the exchange; for its palate has been accustomed to those other sensual pleasures upon which its eyes
are still fixed, and, since the spiritual palate is not made
ready or purged for such subtle pleasure, until it finds itself
becoming prepared for it by means of this arid and dark
night, it cannot experience spiritual pleasure and good, but
only aridity and lack of sweetness, since it misses the pleasure
which aforetime it enjoyed so readily.

5. These souls whom God is beginning to lead through
these solitary places of the wilderness are like to the children
of Israel, to whom in the wilderness God began to give food

---

[3] A, B: 'since it is completely purged as to [its] pleasure.'

from Heaven, containing within itself all sweetness, and, as is there said,[4] it turned to the savour which each one of them desired. But withal the children of Israel felt the lack of the pleasures and delights of the flesh and the onions which they had eaten aforetime in Egypt, the more so because their palate was accustomed to these and took delight in them, rather than in the delicate sweetness of the angelic manna; and they wept and sighed for the fleshpots even in the midst of the food of Heaven.[5] To such depths does the vileness of our desires descend that it makes us to long for our own wretched food[6] and to be nauseated by the indescribable[7] blessings of Heaven.

6. But, as I say, when these aridities proceed from the way of the purgation of sensual desire, although at first the spirit feels no sweetness, for the reasons that we have just given, it feels that it is deriving strength and energy to act from the substance which this inward food gives it, the which food is the beginning of a contemplation that is dark and arid to the senses; which contemplation is secret and hidden from the very person that experiences it; and ordinarily, together with the aridity and emptiness which it causes in the senses, it gives the soul an inclination and desire to be alone and in quietness, without being able to think of any particular thing or having the desire to do so. If those souls to whom this comes to pass knew how to be quiet at this time, and troubled not about performing any kind of action, whether inward or outward, neither had any anxiety about doing anything,[8] then they would delicately experience this inward refreshment in that ease and freedom from care. So delicate is this refreshment that ordinarily, if a man have desire or care[9] to experience it, he experiences it not; for, as I say, it does its work

---

[4] E.p. abbreviates: 'God began to give such delicious food from Heaven that, as is there said.'

[5] Numbers xi, 5–6.

[6] [Lit., 'makes us to desire our miseries.']

[7] [Lit., 'incommunicable.'] E.p. has 'incommutable.'

[8] E.p. reads: '. . . [outward], which they strive with their labour and their reasoning to perform, and had no anxiety to do anything save to allow themselves to be led by God, to receive and to listen with loving interior attentiveness, then . . .' etc.

[9] E.p.: 'if a man have superadded and particular desire and care.'

when the soul is most at ease and freest from care; it is like the air which, if one would close one's hand upon it, escapes.

7. In this sense we may understand that which the Spouse said to the Bride in the Songs, namely: 'Withdraw thine eyes from me, for they make me to soar aloft.'[10] For in such a way does God bring the soul into this state, and by so different a path does He lead it that, if it desires to work with its faculties,[11] it hinders the work which God is doing in it rather than aids it; whereas aforetime it was quite the contrary. The reason is that, in this state of contemplation, which the soul enters when it forsakes meditation for the state of the proficient, it is God Who is now working in the soul; He binds[12] its interior faculties, and allows it not to cling to the understanding, nor to have delight in the will, nor to reason with the memory. For anything that the soul can do of its own accord at this time serves only, as we have said, to hinder inward peace and the work which God is accomplishing in the spirit by means of that aridity of sense. And this peace, being spiritual and delicate, performs a work which is quiet and delicate, solitary, productive of peace and satisfaction[13] and far removed from all those earlier pleasures, which were very palpable and sensual. This is the peace which, says David, God speaks in the soul to the end that He may make it spiritual.[14] And this leads us to the third point.

8. The third sign whereby this purgation of sense may be recognized is that the soul can no longer meditate or reflect in the imaginative sphere of sense as it was wont,[15] however much it may of itself endeavour to do so. For God now begins to communicate Himself to it, no longer through sense, as He did aforetime, by means of reflections which joined and

[10] Canticles vi, 4 [A.V., vi, 5].
[11] E.p.: 'that, if it will work of itself and by its own ability.'
[12] Nearly all authorities read thus. M, e.p., however, have: 'He seems to bind,' and V: 'He veils.'
[13] [Lit., 'satisfactory and pacific.'] E.p. omits: 'solitary, productive of . . . satisfaction.' H has 'solicitous' for 'solitary.' C omits 'solitary.' All other authorities read as in the text.
[14] Psalm lxxxiv, 9 [A.V., lxxxv, 8].
[15] E.p. is slightly explicit: '. . . or reflect, making use of the imaginative sphere of sense, that it may move it as it was wont.'

sundered its knowledge, but by pure spirit, into which con-
secutive reflections enter not; but He communicates Himself
to it by an act of simple contemplation, to which neither the
exterior nor the interior senses of the lower part of the soul
can attain. From this time forward, therefore, imagination
and fancy can find no support in any meditation,[16] and can
gain no foothold by means thereof.

9. With regard to this third sign, it is to be understood that
this embarrassment and dissatisfaction of the faculties proceed
not from indisposition, for, when this is the case, and the
indisposition, which never lasts for long,[17] comes to an end,
the soul is able once again, by taking some trouble about the
matter, to do what it did before, and the faculties find their
wonted support. But in the purgation of the desire this is not
so: when once the soul begins to enter therein, its inability
to reflect with the faculties grows ever greater. For, although
it is true that at first, and with some persons, the process is
not as continuous[18] as this, so that occasionally they fail to
abandon their pleasures and reflections[19] of sense (for perchance[20] by reason of their weakness it was not fitting to wean
them from these immediately), yet this inability grows within
them more and more and brings the workings of sense to an
end, if indeed they are to make progress, for those who walk
not in the way of contemplation act very differently. For this
night of aridities is not usually continuous in their senses. At
times they have these aridities; at others they have them not.
At times they cannot meditate; at others they can. For God
sets them in this night only to prove them and to humble
them, and to reform their desires, so that they go not nurtur-
ing in themselves a sinful[21] gluttony in spiritual things. He
sets them not there in order to lead them in the way of the
spirit, which is this contemplation; for not all those who walk

[16] E.p.: 'cannot find support or make a beginning with any meditation.'
[17] [The stress here is evidently on the transience of the distempers,
whether they be moral or physical.]
[18] Bz.: 'as continent.'
[19] E.p.: 'and alleviation.'
[20] E.p. omits 'perchance.'
[21] E.p. omits: 'a sinful.'

of set purpose in the way of the spirit are brought by God to contemplation, nor even the half of them[22]—why, He best knows. And this is why He never completely weans the senses of such persons from the breasts of meditations and reflections, but only for short periods and at certain seasons, as we have said.

CHAPTER X

Of the way in which these souls are to conduct themselves in this dark night.

DURING the time, then, of the aridities of this night of sense (wherein God effects the change of which we have spoken above, drawing forth the soul from the life of sense into that of the spirit—that is, from meditation to contemplation—wherein it no longer has any power to work or to reason with its faculties concerning the things of God, as has been said), spiritual persons suffer great trials, by reason not so much of the aridities which they suffer, as of the fear which they have of being lost on the road, thinking that all spiritual blessing is over for them and that God has abandoned them since they find no help or pleasure in good things.[1] Then they grow weary, and endeavour (as they have been accustomed to do) to concentrate their faculties with some degree of pleasure upon some object of meditation, thinking that, when they are not doing this and yet are conscious of making an effort, they are doing nothing. This effort they make not without great inward repugnance and unwillingness on the part of their soul, which was taking pleasure in being in that quietness and ease, instead of working with its faculties.[2] So they have abandoned the one pursuit,[3] yet draw no profit from the

---

[22] E.p. reads 'to perfect contemplation' and omits 'nor even the half of them.'

  [1] H: 'no help whatever in good things.'

  [2] E.p. omits: 'instead . . . faculties.'

  [3] [*Lit.*, 'spoiling themselves in the one.'] E.p. has: 'turning aside in [i.e., from] the one.'

other; for, by seeking[4] what is prompted by their own spirit,[5] they lose the spirit of tranquillity and peace[6] which they had before. And thus they are like to one who abandons what he has done in order to do it over again, or to one who leaves a city only to re-enter it, or to one who is hunting and lets his prey go in order to hunt it once more. This is useless here, for the soul will gain nothing further by conducting itself in this way, as has been said.[7]

2. These souls turn back at such a time if there is none who understands them; they abandon the road or lose courage; or, at the least, they are hindered from going farther by the great trouble which they take in advancing along the road of meditation and reasoning. Thus they fatigue and overwork their nature, imagining that they are failing through negligence or sin. But this trouble that they are taking is quite useless, for God is now leading them by another road, which is that of contemplation, and is very different from the first; for the one is of meditation and reasoning, and the other belongs neither to imagination nor yet to reasoning.

3. It is well for those who find themselves in this condition to take comfort, to persevere in patience and to be in no wise afflicted. Let them trust in God, Who abandons not those that seek Him with a simple and right heart, and will not fail to give them what is needful for the road, until He bring them into the clear and pure light of love. This last He will give them by means of that other dark night, that of the spirit, if they merit His bringing them thereto.

4. The way in which they are to conduct themselves in this night of sense is to devote themselves not at all to reasoning and meditation, since this is not the time for it, but to allow the soul to remain in peace and quietness, although it may seem clear[8] to them that they are doing nothing and are wasting their time, and although it may appear to them[9] that

[4] A, B, M, e.p. have 'using.' Bz.: 'tasting.'
[5] [Lit., 'because they seek their spirit.']
[6] G, H, P omit: 'and peace.'
[7] G modifies and abbreviates the rest of the chapter considerably from this point onward.
[8] E.p. omits 'clear.'
[9] E.p. omits: 'although it may appear to them.'

it is because of their weakness that they have no desire in that state to think of anything. The truth is that they will be doing quite sufficient if they have patience and persevere in prayer without making any effort.[10] What they must do is merely to leave the soul free and disencumbered and at rest from all knowledge and thought, troubling not themselves, in that state, about what they shall think or meditate upon, but contenting themselves with merely a peaceful and loving attentiveness toward God, and in being without anxiety, without the ability and without desire[11] to have experience of Him or to perceive Him.[12] For all these yearnings disquiet and distract the soul from the peaceful quiet and sweet ease of contemplation which is here granted to it.

5. And although further scruples may come to them—that they are wasting their time, and that it would be well for them to do something else, because they can neither do nor think anything in prayer—let them suffer these scruples and remain in peace, as there is no question save of their being at ease and having freedom of spirit. For if such a soul should desire to make any effort of its own with its interior faculties, this means that it will hinder and lose the blessings which, by means of that peace and ease of the soul, God is instilling into it and impressing upon it. It is just as if some painter were painting or dyeing a face; if the sitter were to move because he desired to do something, he would prevent the painter from accomplishing anything and would disturb him in what he was doing. And thus, when the soul desires to remain in inward ease and peace, any operation and affection or attention[13] wherein it may then seek to indulge[14] will distract it and disquiet it and make it conscious of aridity

---

[10] [*Lit.*, 'without doing anything themselves.'] E.p. abbreviates: 'persevere in prayer, only leaving the soul free,' etc.

[11] E.p. alters to: 'without excessive desire.' [As in n. 10 above, this edition is endeavouring to soften expressions which might be taken as quietistic.]

[12] E.p.: 'to perceive Him or to have experience of Him.' Bz.: 'to have experience of Him or delight itself in perceiving Him.' [The word rendered 'have experience of' is *gustar*: *lit.*, 'taste.']

[13] E.p.: 'or anxious attention.'

[14] [*Lit.*, 'which it may then wish to have.']

and emptiness of sense. For the more a soul endeavours to find support in affection and knowledge, the more will it feel the lack of these, which cannot now be supplied to it upon that road.

6. Wherefore it behoves such a soul to pay no heed if the operations of its faculties become lost to it; it is rather to desire that this should happen quickly. For, by not hindering the operation of infused contemplation that God is bestowing upon it, it can receive this with more peaceful abundance, and cause[15] its spirit to be enkindled and to burn with the love which this dark and secret[16] contemplation brings with it and sets firmly in the soul.[17] For contemplation is naught else than a secret, peaceful and loving infusion from God, which, if it be permitted, enkindles the soul with the spirit of love, according as the soul declares in the next lines, namely:

Kindled in love with yearnings.[18]

CHAPTER XI

Wherein are expounded the three lines of the stanza.[1]

THIS enkindling of love is not as a rule felt at the first, because it has not begun to take hold upon the soul, by reason of the impurity of human nature, or because the soul has not understood its own state, as we have said, and has therefore given it no peaceful abiding-place within itself. Yet

[15] M, e.p.: 'and be refreshed and cause.'

[16] V: 'and secure.'

[17] E.p. here adds: 'I would not, however, have any general rule laid down here as to cessation from meditation or reflection; for such cessation should never come until meditation is no longer possible, and only when the Lord sets a hindrance to it either in the form of purgation and torment, or in that of most perfect contemplation. At other times, and on other occasions, this support and resource must always be used, and, further [the soul must meditate upon] the life and cross of Christ, which is the best means to purgation and patience, and to security on the road, and a wondrous help to lofty contemplation.'

[18] G departs freely from the text throughout the exposition of this line.

[1] Thus e.p.

sometimes, nevertheless, there soon begins to make itself felt a certain yearning toward God; and the more this increases, the more is the soul affectioned and enkindled in love toward God, without knowing or understanding how and whence this love and affection come to it, but from time to time seeing this flame and this enkindling grow so greatly within it that it desires God with yearning of love; even as David, when he was in this dark night, said of himself in these words,[2] namely: 'Because my heart was enkindled (that is to say, in love of contemplation), my reins also were changed': that is, my desires for sensual affections were changed,[3] namely from the way of sense to the way of the spirit, which is the aridity and cessation from all these things whereof we are speaking. And I, he says, was dissolved in nothing and annihilated, and I knew not; for, as we have said, without knowing the way whereby it goes, the soul finds itself annihilated with respect to all things above and below which were accustomed to please it; and it finds itself enamoured, without knowing how. And because at times the enkindling of love in the spirit grows greater, the yearnings for God become so great in the soul that the very bones seem to be dried up by this thirst, and the natural powers to be fading away, and their warmth and strength to be perishing through the intensity[4] of the thirst of love, for the soul feels that this thirst of love is a living thirst. This thirst David had and felt, when he said: 'My soul thirsted for the living God.'[5] Which is as much as to say: A living thirst was that of my soul. Of this thirst, since it is living, we may say that it kills. But it is to be noted that the vehemence of this thirst is not continuous, but occasional, although as a rule the soul is accustomed to feel it to a certain degree.[6]

[2] Psalm lxxii, 21 [A.V., lxxiii, 21–2].
[3] Thus C, G, H, Mtr., V. The other authorities have only: 'my reins also were changed.' E.p. reads: 'my tastes and affections also were changed,' and continues: 'namely, from the way of sense,' etc.
[4] [Lit., 'livingness': cf. the quotation below.]
[5] Psalm xli, 3 [A.V., xlii, 2].
[6] E.p. substitutes for this last sentence: 'although the vehemence of this thirst is not continuous, but only occasional; howbeit this thirst is ordinarily felt to a certain degree.'

2. But it must be noted that, as I began to say just now, this love is not as a rule felt at first, but only the dryness and emptiness are felt whereof we are speaking. Then in place of this love which afterwards becomes gradually enkindled, what the soul experiences in the midst of these aridities and emptinesses of the faculties is an habitual care and solicitude with respect to God, together with grief and fear that it is not serving Him. But it is a sacrifice which is not a little pleasing to God that the soul should go about afflicted and solicitous for His love. This solicitude and care leads the soul into that secret contemplation, until, the senses (that is, the sensual part) having in course of time been in some degree purged of the natural affections and powers by means of the aridities which it causes within them, this Divine love begins to be enkindled in the spirit. Meanwhile, however, like one who has begun a cure, the soul knows only suffering in this dark and arid purgation of the desire; by this means it becomes healed of many imperfections, and exercises itself in many virtues, in order to make itself meet for the said love, as we shall now say with respect to the line following:

Oh, happy chance!

3. When God leads the soul into this night of sense in order to purge the sense of its lower part and to subdue it, unite it and bring it into conformity with the spirit, by setting it in darkness and causing it to cease from meditation (as He afterwards does in order to purify the spirit to unite it with God, as we shall afterwards say[7]), He brings it into the night of the spirit, and (although it appears not so to it) the soul gains so many benefits that it holds it to be a happy chance to have escaped from the bonds and restrictions of the senses of its lower self, by means of this night aforesaid;[8] and utters the present line, namely: Oh, happy chance! With respect to this, it behoves us here to note the benefits which the soul finds in this night, and because of which it considers it a happy chance to have passed through it; all of which benefits the soul includes in the next line, namely:

[7] E.p. omits: 'as we shall afterwards say.'
[8] E.p.: 'this happy night.'

I went forth without being observed.

4. This going forth is understood of the subjection to its sensual part which the soul suffered when it sought God through operations so weak, so limited and so defective[9] as are those of this lower part; for at every step it stumbled into numerous imperfections and ignorances, as we have noted above in writing of the seven capital sins. From all these it is freed when this night quenches within it all pleasures, whether from above or from below, and makes all meditation darkness to it, and grants it other innumerable blessings in the acquirement of the virtues, as we shall now show. For it will be a matter of great pleasure and great consolation, to one that journeys on this road, to see how that which seems to the soul so severe and adverse, and so contrary to spiritual pleasure, works in it so many blessings. These, as we say, are gained when the soul goes forth, as regards its affection and operation, by means of this night, from all created things, and when it journeys to eternal things,[10] which is great happiness and good fortune:[11] first, because of the great blessing which is in the quenching of the desire and affection with respect to all things; secondly, because they are very few that endure and persevere in entering by this strait gate and by the narrow way which leads to life, as says Our Saviour.[12] The strait gate is this night of sense, and the soul detaches itself from sense and strips itself thereof that it may enter by this gate, and establishes itself in faith,[13] which is a stranger to all sense, so that afterwards it may journey by the narrow way, which is the other night—that of the spirit—and this the soul afterwards[14] enters in order in journey to God in pure faith,[15] which is the means whereby the soul is united to God. By this road, since it is so narrow, dark and terrible (though

[9] E.p. omits: 'so . . . so . . . so . . .'
[10] V: 'to invisible things.'
[11] [Lit., 'and chance': the same word as in the verse-line above.]
[12] St. Matthew vii, 14.
[13] E.p.: 'ruling itself by faith.' Some Codices have: 'uniting itself in faith.'
[14] E.p.: 'later.'
[15] E.p.: 'in faith most pure.'

there is no comparison between this night of sense and that other,[16] in its darkness and trials, as we shall say later), they are far fewer that journey, but its benefits are far greater without comparison than those of this present night. Of these benefits we shall now begin to say something, with such brevity as is possible, in order that we may pass to the other night.

CHAPTER XII

Of the benefits which this night[1] causes in the soul.

THIS night and purgation of the desire, a happy one for the soul, works in it so many blessings and benefits (although to the soul, as we have said, it rather seems that blessings are being taken away from it) that, even as Abraham made a great feast when he weaned his son Isaac,[2] even so is there joy in Heaven because God is now taking this soul from its swaddling clothes, setting it down from His arms, making it to walk upon its feet, and likewise taking from it the milk of the breast and the soft and sweet food proper to children, and making it to eat bread with crust, and to begin to enjoy the food of robust persons. This food, in these aridities and this darkness of sense, is now given to the spirit, which is dry and emptied of all the sweetness of sense. And this food is the infused contemplation whereof we have spoken.

2. This is the first and principal benefit caused by this arid and dark night of contemplation: the knowledge of oneself and of one's misery.[3] For, besides the fact that all the favours which God grants to the soul are habitually granted to them enwrapped in this knowledge, these aridities and this emptiness of the faculties, compared with the abundance

[16] E.p.: 'and that of the spirit.'
[1] E.p.: 'this night of sense.'
[2] Genesis xxi, 8.
[3] So H and the other Codices. E.p. has: 'And this is the first and principal benefit which the soul gains here, and from which almost all the others are derived. Of these, the first benefit is the knowledge of oneself and of one's misery.'

which the soul experienced aforetime and the difficulty which
it finds in good works, make it recognize its own lowliness
and misery, which in the time of its prosperity it was unable
to see. Of this there is a good illustration in the Book of
Exodus, where God, wishing to humble the children of Israel
and desiring that they should know themselves, commanded
them to take away and strip off the festal garments and
adornments wherewith they were accustomed to adorn themselves in the Wilderness, saying: 'Now from henceforth strip
yourselves of festal ornaments and put on everyday working
dress, that ye may know what treatment ye deserve.'[4] This is
as though He had said: Inasmuch as the attire that ye wear,
being proper to festival and rejoicing, causes you to feel less
humble concerning yourselves than ye should, put off from
you this attire, in order that henceforth, seeing yourselves
clothed with vileness, ye may know that ye merit no more, and
may know who ye are. Wherefore the soul knows the truth
that it knew not at first, concerning its own misery; for, at
the time when it was clad as for a festival and found in God
much pleasure, consolation and support, it was somewhat
more satisfied and contented, since it thought itself to some
extent to be serving God. It is true that such souls may not
have this idea explicitly in their minds; but some suggestion
of it at least is implanted in them by the satisfaction which
they find in their pleasant experiences. But, now that the
soul has put on its other and working attire—that of aridity
and abandonment—and now that its first lights have turned
into darkness, it possesses these lights more truly in this virtue
of self-knowledge, which is so excellent and so necessary,[5]
considering itself now as nothing and experiencing no satisfaction in itself; for it sees that it does nothing of itself
neither can do anything. And the smallness of this self-satis-
faction, together with the soul's affliction at not serving God,
is considered and esteemed by God as greater than all the
consolations which the soul formerly experienced and the
works which it wrought, however great they were, inasmuch

[4] Exodus xxxiii, 5.
[5] E.p.: 'it more truly possesses and has this virtue of self-knowledge
so excellent and so necessary.' Our reading is that of H.

as they were the occasion of many imperfections and ignorances. And from this attire[6] of aridity proceed, as from their
fount and source of self-knowledge, not only the things which
we have described already, but also the benefits which we
shall now describe and many more which will have to be
omitted.

3. In the first place, the soul learns to commune with God
with more respect and more courtesy, such as a soul must ever
observe in converse with the Most High. These it knew not in
its prosperous times of comfort and consolation, for that com-
forting favour[7] which it experienced made its craving for God
somewhat bolder than was fitting, and discourteous and ill-
considered.[8] Even so did it happen to Moses, when he perceived that God was speaking to him; blinded[9] by that
pleasure and desire, without further consideration, he would
have made bold to go to Him if God had not commanded
him to stay and put off his shoes. By this incident we are
shown the respect and discretion in detachment of desire
wherewith a man is to commune with God. When Moses
had obeyed in this matter, he became so discreet and so
attentive that the Scripture says that not only did he not
make bold to draw near to God, but that he dared not even
look at Him.[10] For, having taken off the shoes of his desires
and pleasures, he became very conscious of his wretchedness
in the sight of God, as befitted one about to hear the word
of God. Even so likewise the preparation which God granted[11]
to Job in order that he might speak with Him consisted not
in those delights and glories which Job himself reports that
he was wont to have in his God, but in leaving him naked
upon a dung-hill,[12] abandoned and even persecuted by his

    [6] H: 'this labour,' probably in error [trabajo for traje].
    [7] E.p. omits 'comforting [gustoso].' Bz. has: 'that fervour and
comfort [gusto],' Mtr., V: 'that favour and comfort.'
    [8] E.p. 'somewhat bolder and less courteous than was fitting.'
    [9] E.p. has 'carried away' for 'blinded.'
    [10] This is the reading of e.p. Cf. Exodus iii, 6 [P. Silverio reads,
with] other authorities: 'dared not even reflect.'
    [11] E.p.: 'to hear the Divine words. The preparation likewise which
God granted . . .'
    [12] [Job ii, 7–8.]

friends, filled with anguish and bitterness, and the earth covered with worms. And then the Most High God, He that lifts up the poor man from the dung-hill, was pleased to come down and speak with him there face to face, revealing[13] to him the depths and heights[14] of His wisdom, in a way that He had never done in the time of his prosperity.

4. And here we must note another excellent benefit which there is in this night and aridity of the desire of sense, since we have had occasion to speak of it. It is that, in this dark night of the desire (to the end that the words of the Prophet may be fulfilled, namely: 'Thy light shall shine in the darkness'[15]), God will enlighten the soul, giving it knowledge, not only of its lowliness and wretchedness, as we have said, but likewise of the greatness and excellence of God. For, as well as quenching the desires and pleasures and attachments of sense, He cleanses and frees the understanding that it may understand the truth; for pleasure of sense and desire, even though it be for spiritual things, darkens and obstructs the spirit, and furthermore that straitness[16] and aridity of sense enlightens and quickens the understanding, as says Isaias.[17] Vexation makes us to understand how the soul that is empty and disencumbered, as is necessary for His Divine influence, is instructed supernaturally by God in His Divine wisdom, through this dark and arid night of contemplation,[18] as we have said; and this instruction God gave not in those first sweetnesses and joys.

5. This is very well explained by the same prophet Isaias, where he says: 'Whom shall God teach His knowledge, and whom shall He make to understand the hearing?'[19] To those,

[13] E.p.: 'the Most High God, Who lifts up the poor man from the dung-hill, was pleased to communicate Himself to him with greater abundance and sweetness, revealing . . .'

[14] [Lit., 'the deep heights.']

[15] Isaias lviii, 10.

[16] A, B, Bz., C, H read 'appetite' [apetito] for 'straitness' [aprieto], presumably in error.

[17] Isaias xxviii, 19. [The author omits the actual text.]

[18] To translate this passage at all, we must read the Dios cómo of P. Silverio (p. 403, l. 20), which is also found in P. Gerardo and elsewhere, as cómo Dios.

[19] E.p.: 'to hear His word.'

He says, that are weaned from the milk and drawn away from the breasts.[20] Here it is shown that the first milk of spiritual sweetness is no preparation for this Divine influence, neither is there preparation in attachment to the breast of delectable meditations, belonging to the faculties of sense, which gave the soul pleasure; such preparation consists rather in the lack of the one and withdrawal from the other. Inasmuch as, in order to listen to God, the soul needs to stand upright and to be detached, with regard to affection and sense, even as the Prophet says concerning himself, in these words: I will stand upon my watch (this is that detachment of desire) and I will make firm my step (that is, I will not meditate with sense), in order to contemplate (that is, in order to understand that which may come to me from God).[21] So we have now arrived at this, that from this arid night there first of all comes self-knowledge, whence, as from a foundation, rises this other knowledge of God. For which cause Saint Augustine said to God: 'Let me know myself, Lord, and I shall know Thee.'[22] For, as the philosophers say, one extreme can be well known by another.

6. And in order to prove more completely how efficacious is this night of sense, with its aridity and its desolation, in bringing the soul that light which, as we say, it receives there from God, we shall quote that passage of David, wherein he clearly describes the great power which is in this night for bringing the soul this lofty knowledge of God. He says, then, thus: 'In the desert land, waterless, dry and pathless, I appeared before Thee, that I might see Thy virtue and Thy glory.'[23] It is a wondrous thing that David should say here that the means and the preparation for his knowledge of the glory of God were not the spiritual delights and the many pleasures which he had experienced, but the aridities and detachments of his sensual nature, which is here to be understood by the dry and desert land. No less wondrous is it that he should describe as the road to his perception and vision

---

[20] Isaias xxviii, 9.
[21] Habacuc ii, 1.
[22] St. Augustine: *Soliloq.*, Cap. ii.
[23] Psalm lxii, 3 [A.V., lxiii, 1–2].

of the virtue of God, not the Divine meditations and conceptions of which he had often made use, but his being
unable to form any conception of God or to walk by meditation produced by imaginary consideration, which is here to
be understood by the pathless land. So that the means to a
knowledge of God and of oneself is this dark night with its
aridities and voids, although it leads not to a knowledge of
Him of the same plenitude and abundance that comes from
the other night of the spirit, since this is only, as it were, the
beginning of that other.

7. Likewise, from the aridities and voids of this night of
the desire, the soul draws spiritual humility, which is the
contrary virtue to the first capital sin, which, as we said, is
spiritual pride. Through this humility, which is acquired by
the said knowledge of self, the soul is purged from all those
imperfections whereinto it fell with respect to that sin of
pride,[24] in the time of its prosperity. For it sees itself so dry
and miserable that the idea never even occurs to it that it is
making better progress than others, or outstripping them,
as it believed itself to be doing before. On the contrary, it
recognizes that others are making better progress than itself.

8. And hence arises the love of its neighbours, for it
esteems them, and judges them not as it was wont to do
aforetime, when it saw that itself had great fervour and
others not so. It is aware only of its own wretchedness, which
it keeps before its eyes to such an extent that it never forgets
it, nor takes occasion to set its eyes on anyone else. This was
described wonderfully by David, when he was in this night,
in these words: 'I was dumb and was humbled and kept
silence from good things and my sorrow was renewed.'[25] This
he says because it seemed to him that the good that was in
his soul had so completely departed that not only did he
neither speak nor find any language concerning it, but with
respect to the good of others he was likewise dumb because
of his grief at the knowledge of his misery.

9. In this condition, again, souls become submissive and
obedient upon the spiritual road, for, when they see their own

[24] E.p. omits: 'with respect to that sin of pride.'
[25] Psalm xxxviii, 3 [A.V., xxxix, 2].

misery, not only do they hear[26] what is taught them, but they even desire that anyone soever may set them on the way and tell them what they ought to do. The affective[27] presumption which they sometimes had in their prosperity is taken from them; and finally, there are swept away from them on this road all the other imperfections which we noted above with respect to this first sin, which is spiritual pride.[28]

CHAPTER XIII

Of other benefits which this night of sense causes in the soul.[1]

WITH respect to the soul's imperfections of spiritual avarice, because of which it coveted this and that spiritual thing and found no satisfaction in this and that exercise by reason of its covetousness for the desire and pleasure which it found therein, this arid and dark night has now greatly reformed it. For, as it finds not the pleasure and sweetness which it was wont to find, but rather finds affliction and lack of sweetness, it has such moderate recourse to them that it might possibly now lose, through defective use, what aforetime it lost through excess; although as a rule God gives to those whom He leads into this night humility and readiness, albeit with lack of sweetness, so that what is commanded them they may do for God's sake alone; and thus they no longer seek profit in many things[2] because they find no pleasure in them.

2. With respect to spiritual luxury, it is likewise clearly seen that, through this aridity and lack of sensible sweetness which the soul finds in spiritual things, it is freed from those impurities which we there noted; for we said that, as a rule, they proceeded from the pleasure which overflowed from spirit into sense.

---

[26] Bz.: 'do they obey.'

[27] E.p. omits 'affective.'

[28] E.p.: 'all the other imperfections are swept away from them which we touched on above when speaking of spiritual pride.' A, B add: 'as we have said.'

[1] From e.p.

[2] E.p.: 'and thus they detach themselves from many things.'

3. But with regard to the imperfections from which the soul frees itself in this dark night with respect to the fourth sin, which is spiritual gluttony,[3] they may be found above, though they have not all been described there, because they are innumerable; and thus I will not detail them here, for I would fain make an end of this night in order to pass to the next, concerning which we shall have to pronounce grave words and instructions.[4] Let it suffice for the understanding of the innumerable benefits which, over and above those mentioned, the soul gains in this night with respect to this sin[5] of spiritual gluttony, to say that it frees itself from all those imperfections which have there been described, and from many other and greater evils, and vile abominations[6] which are not written above, into which fell many of whom we have had experience, because they had not reformed their desire as concerning this inordinate love of spiritual sweetness. For in this arid and dark night wherein He sets the soul, God has restrained its concupiscence and curbed its desire so that the soul cannot feed upon any pleasure or sweetness of sense,[7] whether from above or from below; and this He continues to do[8] after such manner that the soul is subjected, reformed and repressed with respect to concupiscence and desire. It loses the strength of its passions and concupiscence and it becomes sterile, because it no longer consults its likings. Just as, when none is accustomed to take milk from the breast, the courses of the milk[9] are dried up, so the desires of the soul are dried up. And besides[10] these things there follow admirable benefits from this spiritual sobriety, for,

---

[3] H erroneously reads: 'spiritual pleasure.'

[4] E.p.: 'grave instructions.'

[5] E.p.: 'against this sin.'

[6] E.p. omits: 'and vile abominations.'

[7] E.p.: 'so that it can hardly feed at all upon sweetnesses or pleasures of sense.'

[8] H omits: 'and this He continues to do.'

[9] A: 'of the breast of the milk'; Mtr.: 'of the veins of the milk.'

[10] E.p. omits freely, reading: 'and this He continues to do after such manner that the soul is gradually correcting, mortifying and controlling itself, as regards concupiscence and desire, so that it seems to be losing the strength of its passions; and besides . . .'

when desire and concupiscence are quenched, the soul lives in spiritual tranquillity and peace; for, where desire and concupiscence reign not, there is no disturbance, but peace and consolation of God.

4. From this there arises another and a second benefit, which is that the soul habitually has remembrance of God, with fear and dread of backsliding upon the spiritual road, as has been said. This is a great benefit, and not one of the least that results from this aridity and purgation of the desire, for the soul is purified and cleansed of the imperfections that were clinging to it because of the desires and affections, which of their own accord deaden and darken the soul.

5. There is another very great benefit for the soul in this night, which is that it practices several virtues together, as, for example, patience and longsuffering, which are often called upon in these times of emptiness and aridity, when the soul endures and perseveres in its spiritual exercises without consolation and without pleasure. It practises the charity of God, since it is not now moved by the pleasure of attraction and sweetness which it finds in its work, but only by God. It likewise practises here the virtue of fortitude, because, in these difficulties and insipidities which it finds in its work, it brings strength out of weakness and thus becomes strong. All the virtues, in short—the theological and also the cardinal and moral—both in body and in spirit,[11] are practised by the soul in these times of aridity.

6. And that in this night the soul obtains these four benefits which we have here described (namely, delight of peace, habitual remembrance and thought of God, cleanness and purity of soul and the practice of the virtues which we have just described), David tells us, having experienced it himself when he was in this night, in these words: 'My soul refused consolations, I had remembrance of God, I found consolation and was exercised and my spirit failed.'[12] And he then says: 'And I meditated by night with my heart and

---

[11] E.p. reads: 'All the virtues, the cardinal, and also the theological and moral,' and omits: 'both in body and in spirit.'

[12] Psalm lxxvi, 4 [A.V., lxxvii, 3–4].

was exercised, and I swept and purified my spirit'—that is to say, from all the affections.[13]

7. With respect to the imperfections of the other three spiritual sins which we have described above, which are wrath, envy and sloth, the soul is purged hereof likewise in this aridity of the desire and acquires the virtues opposed to them; for, softened and humbled by these aridities and hardships and other temptations and trials wherein God exercises it during this night, it becomes meek with respect to God, and to itself, and likewise with respect to its neighbour. So that it is no longer disturbed and angry with itself because of its own faults, nor with its neighbour because of his, neither is it displeased with God, nor does it utter unseemly complaints because He does not quickly make it holy.

8. Then, as to envy, the soul has charity toward others in this respect also; for, if it has any envy, this is no longer a vice as it was before, when it was grieved because others were preferred to it and given greater advantage. Its grief now comes from seeing how great is its own misery, and its envy (if it has any) is a virtuous envy, since it desires to imitate others, which is great virtue.

9. Neither are the sloth and the irksomeness which it now experiences concerning spiritual things vicious as they were before. For in the past these sins proceeded from the spiritual pleasures which the soul sometimes experienced and sought after when it found them not. But this new weariness proceeds not from this insufficiency of pleasure, because God has taken from the soul pleasure in all things in this purgation of the desire.

10. Besides these benefits which have been mentioned, the soul attains innumerable others by means of this arid contemplation. For often, in the midst of these times of aridity and hardship, God communicates to the soul, when it is least expecting it, the purest spiritual sweetness and love, together with a spiritual knowledge which is sometimes very delicate, each manifestation of which is of greater benefit and worth than those which the soul enjoyed aforetime; although in its beginnings the soul thinks that this is not so, for the

[13] Psalm lxxvi, 7 [A.V., lxxvii, 6].

spiritual influence now granted to it is very delicate and cannot be perceived by sense.

11. Finally, inasmuch as the soul is now purged from the affections and desires of sense, it obtains liberty of spirit, whereby in ever greater degree it gains the twelve fruits of the Holy Spirit. Here, too, it is wondrously delivered from the hands of its three enemies—devil, world and flesh; for, its pleasure and delight of sense being quenched with respect to all things, neither the devil nor the world nor sensuality has any arms or any strength wherewith to make war upon the spirit.

12. These times of aridity, then, cause the soul to journey in all purity in the love of God, since it is no longer influenced in its actions by the pleasure and sweetness of the actions themselves, as perchance it was when it experienced sweetness, but only by a desire to please God. It becomes neither presumptuous nor self-satisfied, as perchance it was wont to become in the time of its prosperity, but fearful and timid with regard to itself, finding in itself no satisfaction whatsoever; and herein consists that holy fear which preserves and increases the virtues. This aridity, too, quenches natural energy and concupiscence, as has also been said. Save for the pleasure, indeed, which at certain times God Himself infuses into it, it is a wonder if it finds pleasure and consolation of sense, through its own diligence, in any spiritual exercise or action, as has already been said.

13. There grows within souls that experience this arid night concern for God and yearnings to serve Him, for in proportion as the breasts of sensuality, wherewith it sustained and nourished the desires that it pursued, are drying up, there remains nothing in that aridity and detachment save the yearning to serve God, which is a thing very pleasing to God. For, as David says, an afflicted spirit is a sacrifice to God.[14]

14. When the soul, then, knows that, in this arid purgation through which it has passed, it has derived and attained so many and such precious benefits[15] as those which have

[14] Psalm l, 19 [A.V., li, 17].

[15] E.p.: 'attained such precious benefits, and so many.'

here been described, it tarries not in crying, as in the stanza of which we are expounding the lines, 'Oh, happy chance!—I went forth without being observed.' That is, 'I went forth' from the bonds and subjection of the desires of sense and the affections, 'without being observed'—that is to say, without the three enemies aforementioned being able to keep me from it. These enemies, as we have said, bind the soul as with bonds,[16] in its desires and pleasures, and prevent it from going forth from itself to the liberty of the love[17] of God; and without these desires and pleasures they cannot give battle to the soul, as has been said.

15. When, therefore, the four passions of the soul—which are joy, grief, hope and fear—are calmed through continual mortification; when the natural desires have been lulled to sleep, in the sensual nature of the soul, by means of habitual times of aridity; and when the harmony of the senses and the interior faculties causes a suspension of labour and a cessation from the work of meditation, as we have said (which is the dwelling and the household of the lower part of the soul), these enemies cannot obstruct this spiritual liberty, and the house remains at rest and quiet, as says the following line:

My house being now at rest.[18]

CHAPTER XIV

Expounds this last line of the first stanza.[1]

WHEN this house of sensuality was now at rest—that is, was mortified—its passions being quenched and its desires put

[16] E.p. omits: 'as with bonds.'
[17] E.p.: 'of the perfect love.'
[18] [So e.p., which completes the sense of the paragraph. The other versions, which P. Silverio follows, leave it unfinished, reading: '. . . of the soul), which is that which the Lord (*sic*) here calls His house, she says: "My house being now at rest." ']
[1] The title is from e.p. In the first four lines of the first paragraph the Codices show considerable variations in secondary matters. We here follow H.

to rest and lulled to sleep by means of this blessed night of the purgation of sense, the soul went forth, to set out upon the road and way of the spirit, which is that of progressives and proficients,[2] and which, by another name, is called the way of illumination or of infused contemplation, wherein God Himself feeds and refreshes the soul, without meditation, or the soul's active help.[3] Such, as we have said, is the night and purgation of sense in the soul.[4] In those who have afterwards to enter the other and more formidable night of the spirit, in order to pass to the Divine union of love of God (for not all pass habitually thereto, but only the smallest number), it is wont to be accompanied by formidable trials and temptations of sense, which last for a long time, albeit longer in some than in others. For to some the angel of Satan presents himself—namely, the spirit of fornication—that he may buffet their senses with abominable and violent temptations, and trouble their spirits with vile considerations and representations which are most[5] visible to the imagination, which things at times are a greater affliction to them than death.[6]

2. At other times in this night there is added to these things the spirit of blasphemy, which roams abroad, setting in the path of all the conceptions and thoughts of the soul intolerable blasphemies. These it sometimes suggests to the imagination with such violence that the soul almost utters them, which is a grave torment to it.

3. At other times another abominable spirit, which Isaias calls *Spiritus vertiginis*,[7] is allowed to molest them, not in order that they may fall, but that it may try them. This spirit darkens their senses in such a way that it fills them with

---

[2] [*de los aprovechantes y aprovechados.*] E.p., Bz. omit: 'progressives and.'

[3] H: 'or the soul's active way.' The 1630 edition reads as in the text above, but adds: 'with labour.'

[4] E.p. omits: 'in the soul.'

[5] Bz., e.p.: 'are very.'

[6] The next paragraph is lacking in V.

[7] [The 'spirit of giddiness' of D.V., and 'perverse spirit' of A.V., Isaias xix, 14.] E.p. adds: 'is allowed to try them,' and omits: 'not in order that they may fall, but.'

numerous scruples and perplexities, so confusing that, as they judge, they can never, by any means, be satisfied concerning them, neither can they find any help for their judgment[8] in counsel or thought. This is one of the severest goads and horrors of this night, very closely akin to that which passes in the night of the spirit.

4. As a rule these storms and trials are sent by God in this night and purgation of sense to those whom afterwards He purposes to lead into the other night (though not all reach it), to the end that, when they have been chastened and buffeted, they may in this way continually exercise and prepare themselves, and continually accustom their senses and faculties to the union of wisdom which is to be bestowed upon them in that other night. For, if the soul be not tempted, exercised and proved with trials and temptations, it cannot quicken[9] its sense of Wisdom. For this reason it is said in Ecclesiasticus: 'He that has not been tempted, what does he know? And he that has not been proved, what are the things that he recognizes?'[10] To this truth Jeremias bears good witness, saying: 'Thou didst chastise me, Lord, and I was instructed.'[11] And the most proper form of this chastisement, for one who will enter into Wisdom, is that of the interior trials which we are here describing, inasmuch as it is these which most effectively purge sense of all favours and consolations to which it was affected, with natural weakness, and by which the soul is truly humiliated in preparation for the exaltation which it is to experience.

5. For how long a time the soul will be held in this fasting and penance of sense, cannot be said with any certainty; for all do not experience it after one manner, neither do all encounter the same temptations. For this is meted out by the will of God, in conformity with the greater or the smaller degree of imperfection which each soul has to purge away. In

[8] So A. The other authorities [and P. Silverio] read: 'for the judgment.'

[9] So Bz., H, Mtr., P, V. A, B, C, M, e.p. read: 'arrive' [which involves a retranslation: 'its senses cannot arrive at wisdom'—this is not a natural reading in the Spanish].

[10] Ecclesiasticus xxxiv, 9–10.

[11] Jeremias xxxi, 18.

conformity, likewise, with the degree of love of union[12] to which God is pleased to raise it, He will humble it with greater or less intensity or in greater or less time. Those who have the disposition and greater strength to suffer, He purges with greater intensity and more quickly. But those who are very weak are kept for a long time in this night, and these He purges very gently and with slight temptations. Habitually, too, He gives them refreshments of sense so that they may not fall away, and only after a long time do they attain to purity of perfection in this life, some of them never attaining to it at all. Such are neither properly in the night nor properly out of it; for, although they make no progress, yet, in order that they may continue in humility and self-knowledge, God exercises them for certain periods and at certain times[13] in those temptations and aridities; and at other times and seasons He assists them with consolations, lest they should grow faint and return to seek the consolations of the world. Other souls, which are weaker, God Himself accompanies, now appearing to them,[14] now moving farther away, that He may exercise them in His love; for without such turnings away they would not learn to reach God.

6. But the souls which are to pass on to that happy and high estate, the union of love, are wont as a rule to remain for a long time in these aridities and temptations,[15] however quickly God may lead them, as has been seen by experience. It is time, then, to begin to treat of the second night.[16]

[12] E.p.: 'of union of love.'
[13] [Lit., 'for certain days.']
[14] E.p.: 'now disappearing (from them).'
[15] E.p. omits: 'and temptations.'
[16] So end the MSS. A and B add: 'wherein God places the soul.' E.p. substitutes for the last sentence: 'Bringing here, then, this book to a close, let us begin to treat of the second night.' G ends: '. . . aridities and temptations, until God set it in the second night of the spirit, whereof we have next to treat.' Bz. has: 'End of the Night. End of the first night and purgation which is of sense. Laus Deus (sic). That which God wills.' P has: 'Finis. Laus Deo Optimo et Maximo. Es (sic) Deus in nobis agitante calescimus ipso.'

BOOK THE SECOND

*Of the Dark Night of the Spirit.**

CHAPTER I

Which begins to treat of the dark night[1] of the spirit and says at what time it begins.

THE soul which God is about to lead onward is not led by His Majesty into this night of the spirit[2] as soon as it goes forth from the aridities and trials of the first purgation and night of sense; rather it is wont to pass a long time, even years, after leaving the state of beginners, in exercising itself in that of proficients. In this latter state it is like to one that has come forth from a rigorous imprisonment;[3] it goes about the things of God with much greater freedom and satisfaction of the soul, and with more abundant and inward delight than it did[4] at the beginning before it entered the said night. For its imagination and faculties are no longer bound, as they were before, by meditation and anxiety of spirit, since it now very readily finds in its spirit the most serene and loving contemplation and spiritual sweetness without the labour of meditation; although, as the purgation of the soul is not complete (for the principal part thereof, which is that of the spirit, is wanting, without which, owing to the communication that exists between the one part and the other,[5] since the subject is one only, the purgation of sense,

---

* The MSS. vary as to the title. Some have none. B begins: 'Book the Second of the Purgation of the Spirit called Dark Night.'
[1] Thus the Codices. E.p. has: 'the second night.'
[2] So H, P. Bz. has: 'into this night and purgation of the spirit.' E.p.: 'into the union of love.'
[3] [*Lit.*, 'from a narrow prison.']
[4] E.p.: 'than it had.'
[5] [i.e., between sense and spirit.]

however violent it may have been, is not yet complete and perfect), it is never without certain occasional necessities, aridities,[6] darknesses and perils which are sometimes much more intense than those of the past, for they are as tokens and heralds of the coming night of the spirit, and are not of as long duration as will be the night which is to come. For, having passed through a period, or periods, or days of this night and tempest, the soul soon returns to its wonted serenity; and after this manner God purges certain souls which are not to rise to so high a degree of love as are others, bringing them at times, and for short periods, into this night of contemplation and purgation of the spirit, causing night to come upon them[7] and then dawn, and this frequently, so that the words of David may be fulfilled, that He sends His crystal— that is, His contemplation—like morsels;[8] although these morsels of dark contemplation are never as intense as is that terrible night of contemplation which we are to describe, into which, of set purpose, God brings the soul that He may lead it to Divine union.

2. This sweetness, then, and this interior pleasure which we are describing, and which these progressives find and experience in their spirits so easily and so abundantly, is communicated to them in much greater abundance than aforetime, overflowing into their senses more than was usual previously to this purgation of sense; for, inasmuch as the sense is now purer, it can more easily feel the pleasures of the spirit after its manner. As, however, this sensual part of the soul is weak and incapable of experiencing the strong things of the spirit, it follows that these proficients, by reason of this spiritual communication which is made to their sensual part, endure therein many frailties and sufferings and weaknesses of the stomach, and in consequence are fatigued in spirit. For, as the Wise Man says: 'The corruptible body presseth down the soul.'[9] Hence comes it that the communications that are granted to these souls cannot be very strong or very in-

---

[6] E.p. omits: 'occasional necessities.'

[7] A, B, M, e.p. omit: 'upon them.'

[8] Psalm cxlvii, 17 [D.V. and A.V.].

[9] Wisdom ix, 15.

tense or very spiritual, as is required for Divine union with
God, by reason of the weakness and corruption of the sensual
nature which has a part in them. Hence arise the raptures
and trances and dislocations of the bones which always happen when the communications are not purely spiritual—that
is, are not given to the spirit alone, as are those of the perfect
who are purified by the second night of the spirit, and in
whom these raptures and torments of the body no longer exist,
since they are enjoying liberty of spirit, and their senses
are now neither clouded nor transported.

3. And in order that the necessity for such souls to enter
this night of the spirit may be understood, we will here note
certain imperfections and perils which belong to these proficients.

CHAPTER II

*Describes other imperfections¹ which belong to these pro-
ficients.*

THESE proficients have two kinds of imperfection: the one
kind is habitual; the other actual. The habitual imperfections
are the imperfect habits and affections which have remained
all the time in the spirit, and are like roots, to which the purgation of sense has been unable to penetrate. The difference
between the purgation of these and that of this other kind is
the difference between the root and the branch, or between
the removing of a stain which is fresh and one which is
old and of long standing. For, as we said, the purgation of
sense is only the entrance and beginning of contemplation
leading to the purgation of the spirit, which, as we have likewise said,² serves rather to accommodate sense to spirit than
to unite spirit with God. But there still remain in the spirit
the stains of the old man, although the spirit thinks not
that this is so, neither can it perceive them; if these stains

¹ [*Lit.*, 'Continues with other imperfections.'] The Codices read
as in the text; but e.p. has: 'Of certain imperfections.'
² E.p. omits: 'as we have likewise said.'

be not removed with the soap and strong lye of the purgation
of this night, the spirit will be unable to come to the purity
of Divine union.

2. These souls have likewise the *hebetudo mentis*[3] and the
natural roughness which every man contracts through sin, and
the distraction and outward clinging of the spirit, which
must be enlightened, refined and recollected by the afflictions
and perils of that night. These habitual imperfections belong
to all those who have not passed beyond this state of the
proficient; they cannot coexist, as we say,[4] with the perfect
state of union through love.

3. To actual imperfections all are not liable in the same
way. Some, whose spiritual good is[5] so superficial and so
readily affected by sense, fall into greater[6] difficulties and
dangers, which we described at the beginning of this treatise.
For, as they find so many and such abundant spiritual[7] communications and apprehensions, both in sense and in spirit,
wherein they oftentimes see imaginary and spiritual visions
(for all these things, together with other delectable feelings,
come to many souls in this state, wherein the devil and their
own fancy very commonly practise deceptions on them),
and, as the devil is apt to take such pleasure in impressing
upon the soul and suggesting to it the said apprehensions and
feelings, he fascinates and deludes it with great ease,[8] unless
it takes the precaution of resigning itself to God, and of pro-
tecting itself strongly, by means of faith, from all these visions
and feelings. For in this state the devil causes many to believe
in vain visions[9] and false prophecies; and strives[10] to make
them presume that God and the saints are speaking with
them; and they often trust their own fancy. And the devil is
also accustomed, in this state, to fill them with presumption

---

[3] [i.e., 'deadening of the mind.']

[4] E.p. omits: 'as we say.'

[5] Bz.: 'spiritual pleasures are.'

[6] E.p.: 'into certain.'

[7] E.p. omits 'spiritual.'

[8] A, M: 'with great difficulty': presumably a copyist's error.

[9] A, B, M, e.p.: 'causes to be believed many visions.'

[10] So e.p. The Codices [and also, rather meaninglessly, P. Silverio]
read: 'here, in this place, he strives.'

and pride, so that they become attracted by vanity and arrogance, and allow themselves to be seen engaging in outward acts which appear holy, such as raptures and other manifestations. Thus they become bold with God, and lose holy fear, which is the key and the custodian of all the virtues; and in some of these souls so many are the falsehoods and deceits which tend to multiply, and so inveterate do they grow, that it is very doubtful if such souls will return[11] to the pure road of virtue and true spirituality. Into these miseries they fall because they are beginning to give themselves over to spiritual feelings and apprehensions with too great security, when they were beginning to make some progress upon the way.[12]

4. There is much more that I might say of these imperfections and of how they are the more incurable because such souls consider them to be more spiritual than the others, but I will leave this subject. I shall only add, in order to prove how necessary, for him that would go farther, is the night of the spirit, which is purgation, that none of these proficients, however strenuously he may have laboured, is free, at best, from many of those natural affections and imperfect habits, purification from which,[13] we said, is necessary if a soul is to pass to Divine union.

5. And over and above this (as we have said already), inasmuch as the lower part of the soul still has a share in these spiritual communications, they cannot be as intense, as pure and as strong as is needful for the aforesaid union; wherefore, in order to come to this union, the soul must needs enter into the second night of the spirit, wherein it must strip sense and spirit perfectly from all these apprehensions and from all sweetness, and be made to walk in dark and pure faith, which is the proper and adequate means whereby the soul is united with God, according as Osee says, in these words: 'I will betroth thee—that is, I will unite thee—with Me through faith.'[14]

[11] Bz.: 'it is very difficult for such to return.'
[12] E.p.: 'the spiritual way.'
[13] Bz.: 'mortification whereof.'
[14] Osee ii, 20. E.p. has: 'I will betroth thee with Me through faith.'

CHAPTER III

Annotation for that which follows.

THESE souls, then, have now become proficients, because of the time which they have spent in feeding the senses with sweet communications,[1] so that their sensual part, being thus attracted and delighted by spiritual pleasure, which came to it from the spirit, may be united with the spirit and made one with it; each part after its own manner eating of one and the same spiritual food and from one and the same dish, as one person and with one sole intent, so that thus they may in a certain way be united and brought into agreement, and, thus united, may be prepared for the endurance of the stern and severe purgation of the spirit which awaits them. In this purgation these two parts of the soul, the spiritual and the sensual, must be completely purged, since the one is never truly purged without the other, the purgation of sense becoming effective when that of the spirit has fairly begun. Wherefore the night which we have called that of sense may and should be called a kind of correction and restraint of the desire rather than purgation. The reason is that all the imperfections and disorders of the sensual part have their strength and root in the spirit, where all habits, both good and bad, are brought into subjection,[2] and thus, until these are purged, the rebellions and depravities of sense cannot be purged thoroughly.[3]

2. Wherefore, in this night following, both parts of the soul are purged together, and it is for this end that it is well to have passed through the corrections of the first night, and the period of tranquillity[4] which proceeds from it, in order

---

[1] E.p. begins: 'These [souls], then, have now become proficients because of the time which they have spent in experiencing these sweet commmunications.'

[2] E.p. omits: 'where . . . subjection.'

[3] E.p.: 'until the bad habits are purged, the rebellions and depravities of sense cannot be purged thoroughly.'

[4] E.p.: 'and to have attained to the period of tranquillity' [*lit.*, 'the fair weather'].

that, sense[5] being united with spirit, both may be purged after a certain manner and may then suffer with greater fortitude. For very great fortitude[6] is needful for so violent and severe a purgation, since, if the weakness of the lower part has not first been corrected and fortitude has not been gained from God through the sweet and delectable communion which the soul has afterwards enjoyed with Him, its nature will not have the strength or the disposition to bear it.

3. Therefore, since these proficients are still at a very low stage of progress, and follow their own nature closely[7] in the intercourse and dealings which they have with God, because the gold of their spirit is not yet purified and refined, they still think of God as little children, and speak of God as little children, and feel and experience God as little children, even as Saint Paul says,[8] because they have not reached perfection, which is the union of the soul[9] with God. In the state of union, however, they will work great things in[10] the spirit, even as grown men, and their works and faculties will then be Divine rather than human, as will afterwards be said. To this end God is pleased to strip them of this old man and clothe them with the new man, who is created according to God, as the Apostle says,[11] in the newness of sense. He strips their faculties, affections and feelings, both spiritual and sensual, both outward and inward, leaving the understanding dark, the will dry, the memory empty and the affections in the deepest affliction, bitterness and constraint, taking from the soul the pleasure and experience of spiritual blessings which it had aforetime, in order to make of this privation one of the principles which are requisite in the spirit so that there may be introduced into it and united with it the spiritual form of the spirit, which is the union of love. All this the Lord works in the soul by means of a pure

---

[5] Only Bz., H, Mtr., V have the word 'sense.'

[6] Most authorities omit 'fortitude' [which, however, the context supplies]. Bz. gives it explicitly; A has: 'great preparation.'

[7] E.p. omits: 'and . . . closely.'

[8] 1 Corinthians xiii, 11.

[9] E.p.: 'the union of love.'

[10] A, B, M, e.p. have 'with' for 'in.'

[11] [Ephesians iv, 24.]

and dark contemplation,[12] as the soul explains in the first stanza. This, although we originally[13] interpreted it with reference to the first night of sense, is principally understood by the soul of this second night of the spirit, since this is the principal part of the purification of the soul. And thus we shall set it down and expound it here again in this sense.

CHAPTER IV

Sets down the first stanza and the exposition thereof.[1]

On a dark night, Kindled[2] in love with yearnings—
oh, happy chance!—
I went forth without being observed, My house being
now at rest.

EXPOSITION[3]

INTERPRETING this stanza now with reference to purgation, contemplation or detachment or poverty of spirit, which here are almost one and the same thing, we can expound it after this manner and make the soul speak thus: In poverty, and without protection[4] or support in all the apprehensions of my soul—that is, in the darkness of my understanding and the constraint of my will, in affliction and anguish with respect to memory, remaining in the dark in pure faith, which is dark night for the said natural faculties, the will alone being touched by grief and afflictions and yearnings for the love of God—I went forth from myself—that is, from my low manner of understanding, from my weak mode of loving and

---

[12] Bz.: 'of a dark and clean contemplation.'
[13] Only e.p. has: 'originally.'
[1] So e.p. The Codices have only 'Stanza the First' or no title at all. V reads: 'Stanza for the third part.'
[2] B, G, H, M: 'aflame.'
[3] Omitted by A, B, e.p.
[4] E.p. omits: 'protection or.'

from my poor and limited manner of experiencing God, without being hindered therein by sensuality or the devil.

2. This was a great happiness and a good chance for me; for, when the faculties had been perfectly annihilated and calmed, together with the passions, desires[5] and affections of my soul, wherewith I had experienced and tasted God after a lowly manner, I went forth from my own human dealings and operations to the operations and dealings of God.[6] That is to say, my understanding went forth from itself, turning from the human and natural to the Divine; for, when it is united with God by means of this purgation, its understanding no longer comes through its natural light and vigour,[7] but through the Divine Wisdom wherewith it has become united. And my will went forth from itself, becoming Divine; for, being united with Divine love, it no longer loves with its natural strength after a lowly manner,[8] but with strength and purity from the Holy Spirit;[9] and thus the will, which is now near to God, acts not after a human manner, and similarly the memory has become transformed into eternal apprehensions of glory. And finally, by means of this night and purgation of the old man, all the energies and affections of the soul are wholly renewed into a Divine temper and Divine delight.

There follows the line:

On a dark night.

[5] E.p. omits 'desires.'

[6] E.p.: 'I went forth from the dealings and limited operations aforementioned to the operations and dealings of God.'

[7] E.p.: 'it no longer has understanding after the narrow and limited manner that it had aforetime.'

[8] E.p.: 'comes with the limited vigour and strength that it had aforetime.'

[9] E.p.: 'from the Divine Spirit.'

CHAPTER V

Sets down the first line and begins to explain how this dark contemplation is not only night for the soul but is also grief and torment.[1]

THIS dark night is an inflowing of God into the soul, which purges it from its ignorances and imperfections, habitual, natural and spiritual, and which is called by contemplatives infused contemplation, or mystical theology. Herein God secretly teaches the soul and instructs it in perfection of love, without its doing anything, or understanding of what manner is this infused contemplation.[2] Inasmuch as it is the loving wisdom of God, God produces striking effects[3] in the soul, for, by purging and illumining it, He prepares it for the union of love with God. Wherefore the same loving wisdom that purges[4] the blessed spirits and enlightens them is that which here purges the soul and illumines it.

2. But the question arises: Why is the Divine light (which, as we say, illumines and purges the soul from its ignorances) here called by the soul a dark night? To this the answer is that for two reasons[5] this Divine wisdom is not only night and darkness for the soul, but is likewise affliction and torment. The first is because of the height of Divine Wisdom, which transcends the talent of the soul, and in this way is darkness to it; the second, because of its vileness and impurity, in which respect it is painful and afflictive to it, and is also dark.

3. In order to prove the first point, we must here assume a certain doctrine of the philosopher, which says that, the clearer and more manifest are Divine things in themselves, the darker and more hidden are they to the soul naturally; just

[1] So e.p. The Codices have no title.
[2] E.p.: 'without its doing any more than wait lovingly upon God, hear Him and receive His light, without understanding of what manner is this infused contemplation.'
[3] E.p.: '. . . of God, it produces special effects.'
[4] A, B, M: 'Wherefore the same wisdom, as a thing that purges.'
[5] So A, B, Bz. The other authorities have: 'for two things.'

as, the clearer is the light, the more it blinds and darkens the pupil of the owl, and, the more directly we look at the sun, the greater is the darkness which it causes in our visual faculty, overcoming and overwhelming it through its own weakness. In the same way, when this Divine light of contemplation assails the soul which is not yet wholly enlightened, it causes spiritual darkness in it; for not only does it overcome it, but likewise it overwhelms it and darkens the act of its natural intelligence. For this reason Saint Dionysius and other mystical theologians call this infused contemplation a ray of darkness—that is to say, for the soul that is not enlightened and purged—for the natural strength of the intellect is transcended and overwhelmed by its great supernatural light. Wherefore David likewise said: That near to God and round about Him are darkness and cloud;[6] not that this is so in fact, but that it is so to our weak understanding, which is blinded and darkened by so vast a light, to which it cannot attain.[7] For this cause the same David then explained himself, saying: 'Through the great splendour of His presence passed clouds'[8]—that is, between God and our understanding. And it is for this cause that, when God sends it out from Himself to the soul that is not yet transformed, this illumining ray[9] of His secret wisdom causes[10] thick darkness in the understanding.

4. And it is clear that this dark contemplation is in these its beginnings painful likewise to the soul; for, as this Divine infused contemplation has many excellences that are extremely good, and the soul that receives them, not being purged, has many miseries that are likewise extremely bad,[11] hence it follows that, as two contraries cannot coexist in one subject—the soul—it must of necessity have pain and suffering, since it is the subject wherein these two contraries war against each other, working the one against the other, by

---

[6] Psalm xcvi, 2 [A.V., xcvii, 2].

[7] [Lit., 'not attaining.'] B, Bz.: 'not attaining to it.' E.p.: 'not attaining to so great a height.'

[8] Psalm xvii, 13 [A.V., xviii, 12].

[9] H has 'kingdom' for 'ray' [reino for rayo], an evident error.

[10] So e.p. The other authorities [and P. Silverio] read: 'produces.'

[11] E.p. omits: 'that . . . bad.'

reason of the purgation of the imperfections of the soul which comes to pass through this contemplation. This we shall prove inductively in the manner following.

5. In the first place, because the light and wisdom of this contemplation is most bright and pure, and the soul which it assails is dark and impure, it follows that the soul suffers great pain when it receives it in itself, just as, when[12] the eyes are dimmed by humours, and become impure and weak, the assault made upon them by a bright light causes them pain. And when the soul suffers the direct assault of this Divine light, its pain, which results from its impurity, is immense; because, when this pure light assails the soul, in order to expel its impurity, the soul feels itself to be so impure and miserable that it believes God to be against it, and thinks that it has set itself up against God. This causes it sore grief and pain, because it now believes that God has cast it away: this was one of the greatest trials which Job felt when God sent him this experience, and he said: 'Why hast Thou set me contrary to Thee, so that I am grievous and burdensome to myself?'[13] For, by means of this pure light,[14] the soul now sees its impurity clearly (although darkly), and knows clearly that it is unworthy of God or of any creature. And what gives it most pain is that it thinks that it will never be worthy[15] and that its good things are all over for it. This is caused by the profound immersion of its spirit in the knowledge and realization of its evils and miseries; for this Divine and dark light now reveals them all to the eye, that it may see clearly how in its own strength it can never have aught else. In this sense we may understand that passage from David, which says: 'For iniquity Thou hast corrected man and hast made his soul to be undone and consumed: he wastes away as the spider.'[16]

6. The second way in which the soul suffers pain is by

[12] E.p.: 'it follows that to receive it afflicts the soul greatly, even as when,' etc.

[13] Job vii, 20.

[14] Thus the Codices, except A, B, P, which read: 'this clear light.' E.p. has: 'this clear and pure light.'

[15] E.p.: 'is the fear that it will never be worthy.'

[16] Psalm xxxviii, 12 [A.V., xxxix, 11].

reason of its weakness, natural, moral and spiritual; for, when this Divine contemplation assails the soul with a certain force, in order to strengthen it and subdue it, it suffers such pain in its weakness that it nearly swoons away. This is especially so at certain times when it is assailed with somewhat greater force; for sense and spirit, as if beneath some immense and dark load, are in such great pain and agony that the soul would find advantage and relief in death. This had been experienced by the prophet Job, when he said: 'I desire not that He should have intercourse with me in great strength, lest He oppress me with the weight of His greatness.'[17]

7. Beneath the power of this oppression and weight the soul feels itself so far from being favoured that it thinks, and correctly so, that even that wherein it was wont to find some help has vanished with everything else, and that there is none who has pity upon it. To this effect Job says likewise: 'Have pity upon me, have pity upon me,[18] at least ye my friends, because the hand of the Lord has touched me.'[19] A thing of great wonder and pity is it that the soul's weakness and impurity should now be so great that, though the hand of God is of itself so light and gentle, the soul should now feel it to be so heavy and so contrary,[20] though it neither weighs it down nor rests upon it, but only touches it, and that mercifully, since He does this in order to grant the soul favours and not to chastise it.

CHAPTER VI

Of other kinds of pain that the soul suffers in this night.[1]

THE third kind of suffering and pain that the soul endures in this state results from the fact that two other extremes meet here in one, namely, the Divine and the human. The Divine is this purgative contemplation, and the human is the

[17] Job xxiii, 6.
[18] Some Codices do not repeat this phrase.
[19] Job xix, 21.
[20] [There is a reference here to Job vii, 20: cf. § 5, above.]
[1] So e.p. The other authorities have no title.

subject—that is, the soul. The Divine assails the soul in order to renew it[2] and thus to make it Divine; and, stripping it of the habitual affections and attachments of the old man, to which it is very closely united, knit together and conformed, destroys and consumes its spiritual substance,[3] and absorbs it in deep and profound darkness. As a result of this, the soul feels itself to be perishing and melting away, in the presence and sight of its miseries, in a cruel spiritual death, even as if it had been swallowed by a beast and felt itself being devoured in the darkness of its belly, suffering such anguish as was endured by Jonas in the belly of that beast of the sea.[4] For in this sepulchre of dark death it must needs abide until the spiritual resurrection which it hopes for.

2. A description of this suffering and pain, although in truth it transcends all description, is given by David, when he says: 'The lamentations of death compassed me about; the pains of hell surrounded me; I cried in my tribulation.'[5] But what the sorrowful soul feels most in this condition is its clear perception, as it thinks, that God has abandoned it, and, in His abhorrence of it, has flung it into darkness; it is a grave and piteous grief for it to believe that God has forsaken it. It is this that David also felt so much in a like case, saying: 'After the manner wherein the wounded are dead in the sepulchres,'[6] being now cast off by Thy hand, so that Thou rememberest them no more, even so have they set me in the deepest and lowest lake, in the dark places and in the shadow of death, and Thy fury is confirmed upon me and all Thy waves Thou hast brought in upon me.'[7] For indeed, when this purgative contemplation is most severe, the

---

[2] So H, V. A, B: 'purge it and renew it.' M: 'make it and renew it.' C, P: 'take it and renew it.' Bz.: 'cut it and renew it.' E.p.: 'season it and renew it.' As will be seen, there is a reading for every preference. We cannot be sure which is the true one.

[3] E.p. omits: 'its spiritual substance' and reads: 'breaks it up and bruises it.' The two verbs are greatly varied by the different authorities but their general sense remains much as in the text above, which gives the reading of H, Mtr., V.

[4] Jonas ii, 1.

[5] Psalm xvii, 5–7 [A.V., xviii, 4–5].

[6] H omits: 'in the sepulchres.'

[7] Psalm lxxxvii, 6–8 [A.V., lxxxviii, 5–7].

soul feels very keenly the shadow of death and the lamentations of death[8] and the pains of hell, which consist in its
feeling itself to be without God, and chastised and cast out,
and unworthy of Him;[9] and it feels that He is wroth with it.
All this is felt by the soul in this condition—yea, and more,
for it believes[10] that it is so with it for ever.

3. It feels, too, that all creatures have forsaken it, and that
it is contemned by them, particularly by its friends. Wherefore
David presently continues, saying: 'Thou hast put far from
me my friends and acquaintances; they have counted me an
abomination.'[11] To all this will Jonas testify, as one who likewise experienced it in the belly of the beast, both bodily and
spiritually. 'Thou hast cast me forth (he says) into the deep,
into the heart of the sea, and the flood hath compassed
me; all its billows and waves have passed over me. And I
said, "I am cast away out of the sight of Thine eyes, but I
shall once again see Thy holy temple" (which he says, because God purifies the soul in this state that it may see His
temple); the waters[12] compassed me, even to the soul, the
deep hath closed me round about, the ocean hath covered my
head; I went down to the lowest parts of the mountains;
the bars of the earth have shut me up[13] for ever.'[14] By these
bars are here understood, in this sense, imperfections of the
soul, which have impeded it from enjoying this delectable
contemplation.

4. The fourth kind of pain is caused in the soul by another
excellence of this dark contemplation, which is its majesty
and greatness,[15] from which arises in the soul a consciousness

[8] E.p. omits: 'of death.'

[9] E.p.: 'and He is angered with it.'

[10] E.p. adds: 'with a fearful apprehension,' but no MS. has this
addition.

[11] Psalm lxxxvii, 9 [A.V., lxxxviii, 8].

[12] Bz.: 'the afflictions.'

[13] V: 'surrounded me.'

[14] Jonas ii, 4–7 [A.V., ii, 3–6].

[15] So Bz., C, G, H, Mtr., V. A, B, M omit this phrase. E.p. has:
'which is the majesty and greatness of God.' The Saint may mean
that the soul acquires in this contemplation a greater knowledge of
its own excellence, and in consequence has the greater obligation to
God, in Whose image and likeness it is made.

of the other extreme which is in itself—namely, that of the deepest poverty and wretchedness: this is one of the chiefest pains that it suffers in this purgation. For it feels within itself a profound emptiness and impoverishment of three kinds of good, which are ordained for the pleasure of the soul, which are the temporal, the natural and the spiritual; and finds itself set in the midst of the evils contrary to these, namely, miseries of imperfection, aridity and emptiness of the apprehensions of the faculties and abandonment of the spirit in darkness. Inasmuch as God here purges the soul according to the substance of its sense and spirit, and according to the interior and exterior faculties, the soul must needs be in all its parts reduced to a state of emptiness, poverty and abandonment and must be left dry and empty and in darkness.[16] For the sensual part is purified in aridity, the faculties are purified in the emptiness of their perceptions and the spirit is purified in thick darkness.

5. All this God brings to pass by means of this dark contemplation; wherein the soul not only suffers this emptiness and the suspension of these natural supports and perceptions, which is a most afflictive suffering (as if a man were suspended or held in the air so that he could not breathe), but likewise He is purging the soul, annihilating it, emptying it or consuming in it (even as fire consumes the mouldiness and the rust of metal) all the affections and imperfect habits which it has contracted in its whole life. Since these are deeply rooted in the substance of the soul, it is wont to suffer great undoing[17] and inward torment, besides the said poverty and emptiness, natural and spiritual, so that there may here be fulfilled that passage from Ezechiel which says: 'Heap together the bones and I will burn them in the fire; the flesh shall be consumed and the whole composition shall be burned and the bones shall be destroyed.'[18] Herein is understood the pain which is suffered in the emptiness and poverty of the

[16] Bz.: 'and in black darkness.'

[17] A, B, M: 'great burdens and undoing'; Bz.: 'great sorrow.' The text follows e.p., H, Mtr., P, V.

[18] Ezechiel xxiv, 10.

substance of the soul[19] both in sense and in spirit. And concerning this he then says: 'Set it also empty upon the coals, that its metal may become hot and molten, and its uncleanness may be destroyed within it, and its rust may be consumed.'[20] Herein is described the grave suffering which the soul here endures in the purgation of the fire of this contemplation, for the Prophet says here that, in order for the rust of the affections which are within the soul to be purified and destroyed, it is needful that, in a certain manner, the soul itself should be annihilated and destroyed, since these passions and imperfections have become natural to it.[21]

6. Wherefore, because the soul is purified in this furnace like gold in a crucible, as says the Wise Man,[22] it is conscious of this complete undoing of itself in its very substance, together with the direst poverty, wherein it is, as it were, nearing its end, as may be seen by that which David says of himself in this respect, in these words: 'Save me, Lord (he cries to God), for the waters have come in even unto my soul; I am made fast in the mire of the deep and there is no place where I can stand; I am come into the depth of the sea and a tempest hath overwhelmed me; I have laboured crying, my throat[23] has become hoarse, mine eyes have failed whilst I hope in my God.'[24] Here God greatly humbles the soul in order that He may afterwards greatly exalt it; and if He ordained not that, when these feelings arise within the soul, they should speedily be stilled, it would die[25] in a very short space; but there are only occasional periods when it is conscious of their greatest intensity. At times, however, they are so keen that the soul seems to be seeing hell and perdition opened. Of such are they that in truth go down alive into hell, being purged here on earth in the same man-

[19] E.p.: 'and poverty of the soul.'
[20] Ezechiel xxiv, 11.
[21] Bz.: 'eradicated from it.'
[22] Wisdom iii, 6.
[23] So e.p. The other authorities use the plural form of 'throat' (gargantas).
[24] Psalm lxviii, 2–4 [A.V., lxix, 1–3].
[25] E.p.: 'it would forsake the body.'

ner as there,[26] since this purgation is that which would have to be accomplished there.[27] And thus the soul that passes through this[28] either enters not that place[29] at all, or tarries there but for a very[30] short time; for one hour of purgation here is more profitable than are many there.

CHAPTER VII

Continues the same matter and considers other afflictions and constraints of the will.[1]

THE afflictions and constraints of the will are now very great likewise, and of such a kind that they sometimes transpierce the soul with a sudden remembrance of the evils in the midst of which it finds itself, and with the uncertainty of finding a remedy for them. And to this is added the remembrance of times of prosperity now past; for as a rule souls that enter this night have had many consolations[2] from God, and have rendered Him many services, and it causes them the greater grief to see that they are far removed from that happiness, and unable to enter into it. This was also described by Job, who had had experience of it, in these words: 'I, who was wont to be wealthy and rich, am suddenly undone and broken to pieces; He hath taken me by my neck; He hath broken me and set me up for His mark[3] to wound me; He hath compassed me round about with His lances; He hath wounded all my loins; He hath not spared; He hath poured out my bowels on the earth; He hath broken me with wound upon

[26] E.p.: 'being purged here in a kind of purgatory.' [This reading makes explicit what is evidently meant, the word 'hell,' as the preceding sentence shows, being used metaphorically—a 'concealed' quotation from Psalm liv, 16 (A.V., lv, 15).]

[27] E.p. adds: 'when it is for sins, even though they be venial.'

[28] E.p. adds: 'and is thoroughly purged.'

[29] [i.e., purgatory.]

[30] E.p. omits 'very.'

[1] So e.p. The Codices have no title.

[2] The noun occurs only in e.p.

[3] E.p.: 'for His target.'

wound;[4] He hath assailed me as a strong giant; I have sewed
sackcloth upon my skin and have covered my flesh with ashes;
my face is become swollen with weeping and mine eyes are
blinded.'[5]

2. So many and so grievous[6] are the afflictions of this night,
and so many passages of Scripture are there which could be
cited to this purpose, that time and strength would fail us
to write of them, for all that can be said thereof is certainly
less than the truth. From the passages already quoted some
idea may be gained of them. And, that we may bring the exposition of this line to a close and explain more fully what
is worked in the soul by this night, I shall tell what Jeremias
felt about it, which, since there is so much of it, he describes
and bewails in many words after this manner: 'I am the man
that see my poverty in the rod of His indignation; He hath
threatened me and brought me into darkness and not into
light. So far hath He turned against me and hath converted
His hand upon me all the day! My skin and my flesh hath
He made old; He hath broken my bones; He hath made a
fence around me and compassed me with gall and trial; He
hath set me in dark places, as those that are dead for ever.
He hath made a fence around me and against me, that I may
not go out; He hath made my captivity heavy. Yea, and when
I have cried[7] and have entreated, He hath shut out my
prayer. He hath enclosed my paths and ways out with square
stones; He hath thwarted my steps. He hath set ambushes[8]
for me; He hath become to me a lion in a secret place. He
hath turned aside my steps and broken me in pieces, He hath
made[9] me desolate; He hath bent His bow and set me as a
mark for His arrow. He hath shot into my reins the daughters
of His quiver. I have become a derision to all the people,
and laughter and scorn for them all the day. He hath filled
me with bitterness and hath made me drunken with worm-

---

[4] E.p.: 'He hath broken me and added wounds upon wounds.'
[5] Job xvi, 13–17 [A.V., xvi, 12–16].
[6] A, B, e.p.: 'and so great.'
[7] E.p.: 'when I am calling.'
[8] H, M read: 'bear [sic] ambushes' [cf. Lamentations iii, 10].
[9] E.p.: 'hath left.'

wood. He hath broken my teeth by number;[10] He hath fed me with ashes. My soul is cast out from peace; I have forgotten good things. And I said: "Mine end is frustrated and cut short, together with my desire and my hope from the Lord. Remember my poverty and my excess, the wormwood and the gall. I shall be mindful with remembrance and my soul shall be undone within me in pains." '[11]

3. All these complaints Jeremias makes about these pains and trials, and by means of them he most vividly depicts the sufferings of the soul in this spiritual night and purgation.[12] Wherefore the soul that God sets in this tempestuous[13] and horrible night is deserving of great compassion. For, although it experiences much happiness by reason of the great blessings that must arise on this account within it, when, as Job says, God raises up profound blessings in the soul out of darkness, and brings up to light the shadow of death,[14] so that, as David says, His light comes to be as was His darkness;[15] yet notwithstanding, by reason of the dreadful pain which the soul is suffering, and of the great uncertainty which it has concerning the remedy for it, since it believes,[16] as this prophet says here, that its evil will never end, and it thinks, as David says likewise, that God set it in dark places like those that are dead,[17] and for this reason brought its spirit within it into anguish and troubled its heart,[18] it suffers great pain and grief, since there is added to all this (because of the solitude and abandonment caused in it by this dark night) the fact that it finds no consolation or support in any instruction nor in a spiritual master. For, although in many ways its director may show it good reason for being comforted because of the blessings which are contained in these afflictions, it cannot believe him. For it is so greatly absorbed and im-

[10] E.p. [more exactly]: 'one by one.'
[11] Lamentations iii, 1–20.
[12] E.p.: 'wherein this spiritual night and purgation sets it.'
[13] E.p.: 'fearful.'
[14] Job xii, 22.
[15] Psalm cxxxviii, 12 [A.V., cxxxix, 12].
[16] E.p.: 'it thinks.'
[17] [Lit., 'like to the dead of the world (or of the age).']
[18] Psalm cxlii, 3 [A.V., cxliii, 3–4].

mersed in the realization of those evils wherein it sees its own miseries so clearly, that it thinks that, as its director observes not that which it sees and feels, he is speaking in this manner because he understands it not; and so, instead of comfort, it rather receives fresh affliction, since it believes that its director's advice contains no remedy for its troubles. And, in truth, this is so; for, until the Lord shall have completely purged it after the manner that He wills, no means or remedy is of any service or profit for the relief of its affliction; the more so because the soul is as powerless in this case as one who has been imprisoned in a dark dungeon, and is bound hand and foot, and can neither move nor see, nor feel any favour whether from above or from below, until the spirit is humbled, softened and purified, and grows so keen and delicate and pure that it can become one with the Spirit of God, according to the degree of union of love which His mercy is pleased to grant it; in proportion to this the purgation[19] is of greater or less severity and of greater or less duration.

4. But, if it is to be really effectual, it will last for some years, however severe it be; since the purgative process allows intervals of relief,[20] wherein, by the dispensation of God, this dark contemplation ceases to assail the soul in the form and manner of purgation, and assails it after an illuminative and a loving manner, wherein the soul, like one that has gone forth from this dungeon and imprisonment, and is brought into the recreation of spaciousness and liberty, feels and experiences great sweetness of peace and loving friendship with God, together with a ready abundance of spiritual communication. This is to the soul a sign of the health which is being wrought within it by the said purgation and a foretaste of the abundance for which it hopes. Occasionally this is so great that the soul believes its trials to be at last over. For spiritual things in the soul, when they are most purely spiritual, have this characteristic that, if trials come to it, the soul believes that it will never escape from them, and that all its blessings are now over, as has been seen in the passages

[19] A, B, H, M, P, V have: 'the union.'
[20] A, V, e.p.: 'intervals and reliefs.'

quoted; and, if spiritual blessings come, the soul believes in the same way that its troubles are now over, and that blessings will never fail it. This was so with David, when he found himself in the midst of them, as he confesses in these words: 'I said in my abundance: "I shall never be moved." '[21]

5. This happens because the actual possession by the spirit of one of two contrary things itself makes impossible the actual possession and realization of the other contrary thing; this is not so,[22] however, in the sensual part of the soul, because its apprehension is weak. But, as the spirit is not yet completely purged and cleansed from the affections that it has contracted from its lower part, while changing not in so far as it is spirit, it can be moved to further afflictions in so far as these affections sway it.[23] In this way, as we see, David was afterwards moved, and experienced many ills and afflictions, although in the time of his abundance he had thought and said that he would never be moved. Just so is it with the soul in this condition, when it sees itself moved by that abundance of spiritual blessings, and, being unable to see the root of the imperfection and impurity which still remain within it, thinks that its trials are over.

6. This thought, however, comes to the soul but seldom, for, until spiritual purification is complete and perfected, the sweet communication is very rarely so abundant as to conceal from the soul the root which remains hidden, in such a way that the soul can cease to feel that there is something that it lacks within itself or that it has still to do. Thus it cannot completely enjoy that relief, but feels as if one of its enemies were within it, and although this enemy is, as it were, hushed and asleep, it fears that he will come to life again and attack it.[24] And this is what indeed happens, for, when the soul is most secure and least alert,[25] it is dragged

---

[21] Psalm xxix, 7 [A.V., xxx, 6].

[22] E.p.: 'which is not so much so.'

[23] E.p.: 'the affections that its lower part has contracted, although it has greater consistency and firmness, yet, in so far as it is affected by them, it is liable to further afflictions.'

[24] [Lit., 'and play his tricks upon it.']

[25] E.p. omits: 'and least alert.'

down and immersed again in another and a worse[26] degree of affliction which is severer and darker and more grievous than that which is past; and this new affliction will continue for a further period of time, perhaps longer than the first. And the soul once more comes to believe[27] that all its blessings are over for ever. Although it had thought during its first trial that there were no more afflictions which it could suffer, and yet, after the trial was over, it enjoyed great blessings, this experience is not sufficient to take away its belief, during this second degree of trial, that all is now over for it and that it will never again be happy as in the past. For, as I say, this belief, of which the soul is so sure, is caused in it by the actual apprehension of the spirit, which annihilates within it all that is contrary to it.[28]

7. This is the reason why those who lie in purgatory suffer great misgivings as to whether they will ever go forth from it and whether their pains will ever be over.[29] For, although they have the habit of the three theological virtues—faith, hope and charity—the present realization which they have of their afflictions and of their deprivation of God allows them not to enjoy the present blessing and consolation of these virtues. For, although they are able to realize that they have a great love for God, this is no consolation to them, since they cannot think that God loves them or that they are worthy that He should do so; rather, as they see that they are deprived of Him, and left in their own miseries, they think that there is that in themselves which provides a very good reason why they should with perfect justice be abhorred

[26] E.p. omits: 'and a worse.'

[27] E.p.: 'to persuade itself.' H omits: 'than the first. And then the soul once more comes to [believe that].'

[28] E.p. has: 'which annihilates in it [*the soul, not the spirit, as the gender of the Spanish noun shows*] all that can cause it joy.' It then omits the next paragraph as far as the words 'cast out by God for ever.' A, V also make this omission, but not B, as P. Gerardo mistakenly asserts. G omits almost the whole of this chapter.

[29] M, probably in error [*desean* for *de que se han*]: 'and desire their pains to be over.' B reads very similarly [certainly with intention]. P omits: 'and . . . over.'

and cast out by God for ever.[30] And thus, although the soul in this purgation is conscious that it has a great love for God and would give a thousand lives for Him (which is the truth, for in these trials such souls love their God very earnestly), yet this is no relief to it, but rather brings it greater affliction. For it loves Him so much that it cares about naught beside; when, therefore, it sees itself to be so wretched that it cannot believe that God loves it, nor that there is or will ever be reason why He should do so, but rather[31] that there is

[30] B, Bz., C, H, Mtr. all have this long passage on the suffering of the soul in Purgatory. It would be rash, therefore, to deny that St. John of the Cross is its author, [or to suppose, as P. Gerardo did, that he deleted it during a revision of his works]. An admirably constructed synthesis of these questions will be found in B. Belarmino, *De Purgatorio*, Bk. II, chaps. iv, v. He asks if souls in Purgatory are sure of their salvation. This was denied by Luther, and by a number of Catholic writers, who held that, among the afflictions of these souls, the greatest is this very uncertainty; some maintain that, though they have in fact such certainty, they are unaware of it. Belarmino quotes among other authorities Denis the Carthusian, *De quattuor novissimis*, Gerson (Lect. I *De Vita Spirituali*) and John of Rochester (against Luther's 32nd article); these writers claim that, as sin which is venial is only so through the Divine mercy, it may with perfect justice be rewarded by eternal punishment, and thus souls that have committed venial sin cannot be confident of their salvation. He also shows, however, that the common opinion of theologians is that the souls in Purgatory are sure of their salvation, and considers various degrees of certainty, adding very truly that, while these souls experience no fear, they experience hope, since they have not yet the Beatific vision.

Uncertainty as to their salvation, it is said, might arise from ignorance of the sentence passed upon them by the Judge or from the deadening of their faculties by the torments which they are suffering. Belarmino refutes these and other suppositions with great force and effect. St. John of the Cross seems to be referring to the last named when he writes of the realization of their afflictions and their deprivation of God not allowing them to enjoy the blessings of the theological virtues. It is not surprising if the Saint, not having examined very closely this question, of which he would have read treatments in various authors, thought of it principally as an apt illustration of the purifying and refining effects of passive purgation; and an apt illustration it certainly is.

[31] E.p.: 'when it sees itself to be so miserable, suspecting that God loves it not, and having then no certainty that there is anything in it worthy of love but rather . . .'

reason why it should be abhorred, not only by Him, but by all creatures for ever, it is grieved to see in itself reasons for deserving to be cast out by Him for Whom it has such great love and desire.

CHAPTER VIII

Of other pains which afflict the soul in this state.[1]

But there is another thing here[2] that afflicts and distresses the soul greatly, which is that, as this dark night has hindered its faculties and affections in this way, it is unable to raise[3] its affection or its mind to God, neither can it pray to Him, thinking, as Jeremias thought concerning himself, that God has set a cloud before it through which its prayer cannot pass.[4] For it is this that is meant by that which is said in the passage referred to, namely: 'He hath shut and enclosed my paths with square stones.'[5] And if it sometimes prays it does so with such lack of strength and of sweetness[6] that it thinks that God neither hears it nor pays heed to it, as this Prophet likewise declares in the same passage, saying: 'When I cry and entreat, He hath shut out my prayer.'[7] In truth this is no time for the soul to speak with God; it should rather put its mouth in the dust, as Jeremias says, so that perchance there may come to it some present hope,[8] and it may endure its purgation with patience.[9] It is God Who is passively[10] working here in the soul; wherefore the soul can do nothing. Hence it can neither pray nor pay attention when it is pres-

---

[1] So e.p. The Codices have no title.
[2] E.p.: 'There is in this state another thing.'
[3] E.p. adds here: 'as before.'
[4] Lamentations iii, 44.
[5] [Lamentations iii, 9.] E.p. omits 'shut and' and reads 'roads' for 'paths.'
[6] E.p.: 'with such aridity and lack of sweetness.'
[7] Lamentations iii, 8.
[8] Lamentations iii, 29.
[9] E.p.: In 'truth, this is the time to put, as Jeremias says, its mouth in the dust, enduring its purgation with patience.'
[10] E.p. omits 'passively.'

ent at the Divine offices,[11] much less can it attend to other things and affairs which are temporal. Not only so, but it has likewise such distractions and times of such profound forgetfulness of the memory that frequent periods pass by without its knowing what it has been doing or thinking, or what it is that it is doing or is going to do, neither can it pay attention, although it desire to do so, to anything that occupies it.[12]

2. Inasmuch as not only is the understanding here purged of its light,[13] and the will of its affections, but the memory is also purged of meditation and knowledge, it is well that it be likewise annihilated with respect to all these things, so that that which David says of himself in this purgation may by fulfilled, namely: 'I was annihilated and I knew not.'[14] This unknowing refers[15] to these follies and forgetfulnesses of the memory, which distractions and forgetfulnesses are caused by the interior recollection wherein this contemplation absorbs the soul. For, in order that the soul may be divinely prepared and tempered with its faculties for the Divine union of love, it would be well for it to be first of all absorbed, with all its faculties, in this Divine and dark spiritual light of contemplation, and thus to be withdrawn from all the affections and apprehensions of the creatures, which condition ordinarily[16] continues in proportion to its intensity. And thus, the simpler and the purer is this Divine light in its assault upon the soul, the more does it darken it, void it and annihilate it according to its particular apprehensions and affections, with regard both to things above and to things below; and similarly, the less simple and pure is it in this assault, the less deprivation it causes it and the less dark is it. Now this is a thing that seems incredible, to say that, the

[11] [*Lit.*, 'at the Divine things.'] Thus A, B, C, G, Mtr., P. M, e.p.: 'pay great attention.' H: 'present at the Divine things.' Bz.: 'present with devotion at the Divine things.'

[12] E.p.: 'nor can it be very attentive, although it desire to be so, to anything that it is doing.'

[13] E.p.: 'of its imperfect knowledge.'

[14] Psalm lxxii, 22 [A.V., lxxiii, 22].

[15] E.p.: 'extends.'

[16] So M, e.p. The Codices have 'singularly.'

brighter and purer is supernatural and Divine light, the more it darkens the soul, and that, the less bright and pure is it, the less dark it is to the soul. Yet this may readily be understood[17] if we consider what has been proved above by the dictum of the philosopher—namely, that the brighter and the more manifest in themselves are supernatural things the darker are they to our understanding.[18]

3. And, to the end that this may be understood the more clearly, we shall here set down a similitude referring to common and natural light. We observe that a ray of sunlight which enters through the window is the less clearly visible according as it is the purer and freer from specks, and the more of such specks and motes there are in the air, the brighter is the light to the eye. The reason is that it is not the light itself that is seen; the light is but the means whereby the other things that it strikes are seen, and then it is also seen itself, through its reflection in them; were it not for this, neither it nor they would have been seen. Thus if the ray of sunlight entered through the window of one room and passed out through another on the other side, traversing the room, and if it met nothing on the way, or if there were no specks in the air for it to strike, the room would have no more light than before, neither would the ray of light be visible. In fact, if we consider it carefully, there is more darkness where the ray is, since it absorbs and obscures any other light, and yet it is itself invisible, because, as we have said, there are no visible objects which it can strike.

4. Now this is precisely what this Divine ray of contemplation does in the soul. Assailing it with its Divine light, it transcends the natural power of the soul, and herein it darkens it and deprives it of all natural affections and apprehensions which it apprehended aforetime by means of natural light; and thus it leaves it[19] not only dark, but likewise

[17] The words 'this may readily be understood,' which are necessary to complete the sense of the passage, are only found in e.p. and Mtr.

[18] E.p. omits the next paragraph, doubtless because the same comparison has already been used in the *Ascent of Mount Carmel*, Bk. II, chap. xiv, § 9.

[19] E.p. greatly modifies the first part of this paragraph, thus: 'And thus, the ray of this lofty contemplation assails the soul with

empty, according to its faculties and desires, both spiritual and natural. And, by thus leaving it empty and in darkness, it purges and illumines it with Divine spiritual light, although the soul thinks not that it has this light, but believes itself to be in darkness, even as we have said of the ray of light, which, although it be in the midst of the room, yet, if it be pure and meet nothing on its path, is not visible. With regard, however, to this spiritual light by which the soul is assailed, when it has something to strike—that is, when something spiritual presents itself to be understood, however small a speck it be and whether of perfection or imperfection, or whether it be a judgment of the falsehood or the truth of a thing[20]—it then sees and understands much more clearly than before it was in these dark places. And exactly in the same way it discerns the spiritual light which it has in order that it may readily discern the imperfection which is presented to it; even as, when the ray of which we have spoken, within the room, is dark and not itself visible, if one introduce[21] a hand or any other thing into its path, the hand is then seen and it is realized that that sunlight is present.

5. Wherefore, since this spiritual light is so simple,[22] pure and general, not appropriated or restricted to any particular thing that can be understood, whether natural or Divine (since with respect to all these apprehensions the faculties of the soul are empty and annihilated), it follows that[23] with

---

its Divine light, and, since it transcends the natural power of the soul itself, darkens it and deprives it of all the natural apprehensions and affections which it apprehended aforetime by means of natural light. Whereby it leaves it,' etc.

[20] E.p. has: '. . . even as we have said. But even as the ray of light, if it be pure and have nothing to strike or to meet, is hardly perceived, and when it strikes or reflects is the better seen, even so this spiritual light whereby the soul is assailed, since it is so pure, is not in itself observed or perceived; but when it has something to strike—that is, when some particular thing presents itself to be understood, of perfection, or judgment of the falsehood or truth of a thing,' etc.

[21] E.p.: 'even as when the ray is in itself not perceived, yet, if one introduce,' etc.

[22] H: 'so sensible.'

[23] E.p. omits: 'it follows that.'

great comprehensiveness and readiness the soul discerns and penetrates whatsoever thing presents itself to it, whether it come from above or from below; for which cause the Apostle said: That the spiritual man searches all things, even the deep things of God.[24] For by this general and simple wisdom is understood that which the Holy Spirit says through the Wise Man, namely: That it reaches wheresoever it wills by reason of its purity;[25] that is to say, because it is not restricted to any particular object of the intellect or affection. And this is the characteristic of the spirit that is purged and annihilated with respect to all particular affections and objects of the understanding, that in this state wherein it has pleasure in nothing and understands nothing[26] in particular, but dwells in its emptiness, darkness and obscurity, it is fully prepared to embrace everything to the end that those words of Saint Paul may be fulfilled[27] in it: *Nihil habentes, et omnia possidentes.*[28] For such poverty of spirit as this would deserve such happiness.

CHAPTER IX

How, although this night brings darkness to the spirit, it does so in order to illumine it and give it light.[1]

IT now remains to be said that, although this happy night brings darkness to the spirit, it does so only to give it light in everything; and that, although it humbles it and makes it miserable, it does so only to exalt it and to raise it up; and, although it impoverishes it and empties it of all natural affection and attachment, it does so only that it may enable it to stretch forward, divinely, and thus to have fruition and experience of all things, both above and below, yet to pre-

---

[24] 1 Corinthians ii, 10. [*Lit.*, 'penetrates all things.']
[25] Wisdom vii, 24.
[26] H omits: 'and understands nothing.'
[27] A, M, e.p. add 'mystically.'
[28] 2 Corinthians vi, 10.
[1] So e.p. The Codices have no title.

serve its unrestricted liberty of spirit in them all. For just as the elements, in order that they may have a part in all natural entities and compounds, must have no particular colour, odour or taste, so as to be able to combine with all tastes, odours and colours, just so must the spirit be simple, pure and detached from all kinds of natural affection, whether actual or habitual, to the end that it may be able freely to share in the breadth of spirit of the Divine Wisdom, wherein, through its purity, it has experience of all the sweetness of all things in a certain pre-eminently excellent way.[2] And without this purgation it will be wholly unable to feel or experience the satisfaction of all this abundance of spiritual sweetness. For one single affection remaining in the spirit, or one particular thing to which, actually or habitually, it clings, suffices to hinder it from feeling or experiencing or communicating the delicacy and intimate sweetness of the spirit of love, which contains within itself all sweetness to a most eminent degree.[3]

2. For, even as the children of Israel, solely because they retained one single affection and remembrance—namely, with respect to the fleshpots and the meals which they had tasted in Egypt[4]—could not relish the delicate bread of angels, in the desert, which was the manna, which, as the Divine Scripture says, held sweetness for every taste and turned to the taste that each one desired;[5] even so the spirit cannot succeed in enjoying the delights of the spirit of liberty, according to the desire of the will, if it be still affectioned to any desire, whether actual or habitual, or to particular objects of understanding, or to any other apprehension.[6] The reason for this is that the affections, feelings and apprehensions of the perfect spirit, being Divine,[7] are of another kind and of a very different order from those that are natural.

---

[2] [*Lit.*, 'with a certain eminence of excellence.'] So C, H, M, Mtr., P, V. A, B, e.p.: 'certain kind of excellence.' Bz. omits a line or so here.

[3] [*Lit.*, '. . . sweetness, with great eminence.']

[4] Exodus xvi, 3.

[5] Wisdom xvi, 21.

[6] Thus the Codices. E.p. has: 'any other limited apprehension.'

[7] E.p.: 'being so high and very specially Divine.'

They are pre-eminent,[8] so that, in order both actually and habitually to possess the one, it is needful to expel and annihilate the other, as with two contrary things, which cannot exist together in one person.[9] Therefore it is most fitting and necessary, if the soul is to pass to these great things, that this dark night of contemplation should first of all annihilate and undo it in its meannesses, bringing it into darkness, aridity, affliction and emptiness; for the light which is to be given to it is a Divine light of the highest kind, which transcends all natural light, and which by nature can find no place in the understanding.

3. And thus it is fitting that, if the understanding is to be united with that light and become Divine in the state of perfection, it should first of all be purged and annihilated as to its natural light, and, by means of this dark contemplation, be brought actually into darkness. This darkness should continue for as long as is needful in order to expel and annihilate the habit which the soul has long since formed in its manner of understanding, and the Divine light and illumination will then take its place. And thus, inasmuch as that power of understanding which it had aforetime is natural, it follows that the darkness which it here suffers is profound and horrible and most painful, for this darkness, being felt in the deepest substance of the spirit, seems to be substantial darkness.[10] Similarly, since the affection of love which is to be given to it in the Divine union of love is Divine, and therefore very spiritual, subtle and delicate, and very intimate, transcending every affection and feeling[11] of the will, and every desire thereof, it is fitting that, in order that the will may be able to attain to this Divine affection and most lofty delight, and to feel it and experience it[12] through the union of love, since it is not, in the way of nature, perceptible to the will,[13] it be first of all purged and annihilated in all its affec-

[8] E.p. omits the last three words.
[9] E.p. omits: 'as with . . . person.'
[10] E.p. reads: '. . . painful, for it touches, and is felt in, the depths of the spirit.'
[11] E.p.: 'every natural imperfect affection and feeling.'
[12] E.p. omits: 'feel it and.'
[13] E.p. omits: 'since . . . will.'

tions and feelings, and left in a condition of aridity and constraint, proportionate to the habit of natural affections which
it had before, with respect both to Divine things and to human. Thus, being exhausted, withered and thoroughly tried[14]
in the fire of this dark contemplation, and having driven
away every kind[15] of evil spirit (as with the heart of the fish
which Tobias set on the coals[16]), it may have a simple and
pure disposition, and its palate may be purged and healthy,
so that it may feel the rare and sublime touches of Divine
love, wherein it will see itself divinely transformed, and all
the contrarieties, whether actual or habitual, which it had
aforetime, will be expelled, as we are saying.

4. Moreover, in order to attain the said union to which
this dark night is disposing and leading it, the soul must be
filled and endowed with a certain glorious magnificence in
its communion with God, which includes within itself innumerable blessings springing from delights which exceed all
the abundance that the soul can naturally possess. For by
nature the soul is so weak and impure that it cannot receive
all this. As Isaias says: 'Eye hath not seen, nor ear heard,
neither hath it entered into the heart of man, that which God
hath prepared, etc.'[17] It is meet, then, that the soul be first
of all brought into emptiness and poverty of spirit and purged
from all help, consolation and natural apprehension with
respect to all things, both above and below. In this way,
being empty, it is able indeed to be poor in spirit and freed
from the old man, in order to live that new and blessed life

[14] So H. There are many variants. A: 'that it may be dry and
withered and well proved.' B: 'that it may be dry, withered and
well entangled (sic).' [Probably a copyist's error: entrincada for
extricada, 'wrung.'] Bz.: 'that it may be withered and well bruised.'
C, M, P: 'Thus, exhausted and withered and well wrung.' Mtr.:
'that it may be withered and well wrung.' V: 'that it may be clean
and withered and well wrung.' E.p.: 'Thus, exhausted, withered
and deprived (of every kind, etc.).'

[15] [Lit., 'from every kind.' But see Tobias viii, 2. The 'deprived'
of e.p. gives the best reading of this phrase, but the general sense is
clear from the Scriptural reference.]

[16] Tobias viii, 2.

[17] Isaias lxiv, 4 [1 Corinthians ii, 9]. E.p. adds: 'for those that
love Him.'

which is attained by means of this night, and which is the state of union with God.

5. And because the soul is to attain to the possession of a sense, and of a Divine knowledge, which is very generous and full of sweetness, with respect to things Divine and human, which fall not within the common experience and natural knowledge of the soul (because it looks on them with eyes as different from those of the past as spirit is different from sense[18] and the Divine from the human), the spirit must be straitened[19] and inured to hardships as regards its common and natural experience, and be brought by means of this purgative contemplation into great anguish and affliction, and the memory must be borne far from all agreeable and peaceful knowledge, and have an intimate[20] sense and feeling that it is making a pilgrimage and being a stranger to all things, so that it seems to it that all things are strange and of a different kind from that which they were wont to be. For this night is gradually drawing the spirit away from its ordinary and common experience of things and bringing it nearer the Divine sense, which is a stranger and an alien to all human ways. It seems now to the soul that it is going forth from its very self, with much affliction.[21] At other times it wonders if it is under a charm or a spell, and it goes about marvelling at the things that it sees and hears, which seem to it very strange and rare, though they are the same that it was accustomed to experience aforetime. The reason of this is that the soul is now becoming alien and remote from common sense and knowledge of things, in order that, being annihilated in this respect, it may be informed with the Divine—which belongs rather to the next life than to this.

6. The soul suffers all these afflictive purgations[22] of the

[18] E.p.: 'as the light and grace of the Holy Spirit differ from sense.'
[19] [Lit., 'be made thin.']
[20] E.p.: 'a very intimate.'
[21] A, e.p.: '. . . human ways; so much so that it seems to the soul that it is going out from its very self.' So M, omitting the words 'much so.' B, Bz., C, H, V read as in the text.
[22] A, B, M, Mtr., P: 'all these afflictions and purgations.' Bz., C: 'affective purgations.'

spirit to the end that it may be begotten anew in spiritual
life by means of this Divine inflowing, and in these pangs
may bring forth the spirit of salvation, that the saying of Isaias
may be fulfilled: 'In Thy sight, O Lord, we have conceived,
and we have been as in the pangs of labour, and we have
brought forth the spirit of salvation.'[23] Moreover, since by
means of this contemplative night the soul is prepared for
the attainment of inward peace and tranquillity, which is of
such a kind and so delectable that, as the Scripture[24] says, it
passes all understanding,[25] it behoves the soul to abandon all
its former peace. This was in reality no peace at all, since it
was involved in imperfections; but to the soul aforementioned
it appeared to be so, because it was following its own inclinations, which were for peace. It seemed, indeed, to be a twofold
peace—that is, the soul believed that it had already acquired
the peace of sense and that of spirit, for it found itself to be
full of the spiritual abundance of this peace of sense and of
spirit—as I say, it is still imperfect. First of all, then, it must
be purged of that former peace and disquieted concerning it
and withdrawn from it.[26] Even so was Jeremias when, in the
passage which we quoted from him, he felt and lamented[27]
thus, in order to express the calamities of this night that is past,
saying: 'My soul is withdrawn and removed from peace.'[28]

7. This is a painful disturbance, involving many misgivings, imaginings and strivings which the soul has within itself,
wherein, with the apprehension and realization of the miseries
in which it sees itself, it fancies that it is lost and that its
blessings have gone for ever. Wherefore the spirit experi-

[23] Isaias xxvi, 17–18.
[24] [P. Silverio reads, with] A, B, M: 'the gloss.' [This was probably what the Saint actually wrote.] Bz., C, H, Mtr., P [not understanding it] have: 'the Church' [la Iglesia for la Glosa]. V, e.p.
[give the correct sense by reading]: 'the Scripture.'
[25] [Philippians iv, 7.]
[26] [We have here split up a parenthesis of about seventy words.]
E.p. abbreviates: '[It seemed to be] a twofold peace, that is, of
sense and spirit. First of all it must be purged that it may be disquieted concerning that imperfect peace, and withdrawn from it.'
[27] [Lit., 'and wept.']
[28] Lamentations iii, 17.

ences[29] pain and sighing so deep that they cause it vehement
spiritual groans and cries, to which at times it gives vocal
expression; when it has the necessary strength and power it
dissolves into tears, although this relief comes but seldom.
David[30] describes this very aptly, in a Psalm, as one who has
had experience of it, where he says: 'I was exceedingly afflicted and humbled; I roared with the groaning of my heart.'[31]
This roaring implies great pain; for at times, with the sudden
and acute remembrance of these miseries wherein the soul
sees itself, pain and affliction rise up and surround it, and I
know not how the affections of the soul could be described[32]
save in the similitude of holy Job, when he was in the same
trials, and uttered these words: 'Even as the overflowing of
the waters, even so is my roaring.'[33] For just as at times the
waters make such inundations that they overwhelm and fill
everything, so at times this roaring and this affliction of the
soul grow to such an extent that they overwhelm it and penetrate it completely, filling it with spiritual pain and anguish
in all its deep affections and energies, to an extent surpassing
all possibility of exaggeration.

8. Such is the work wrought in the soul by this night that
hides the hopes of the light of day. With regard to this the
prophet Job says likewise: 'In the night my mouth is pierced
with sorrows and they that feed upon me sleep not.'[34] Now
here by the mouth is understood the will, which is transpierced
with these pains that tear the soul to pieces, neither ceasing
nor sleeping, for the doubts and misgivings which transpierce
the soul in this way never cease.[35]

---

[29] So C, H, Mtr., P, V. The other Codices and e.p. read: 'Wherefore there has entered into the spirit.'

[30] E.p.: 'The royal prophet David.'

[31] Psalm xxxvii, 9 [A.V., xxxviii, 8].

[32] [Lit., '. . . sees itself, it arises and is surrounded with pain and
affliction, the affections of the soul, that I know not how it could
be described.' A confused, ungrammatical sentence, of which, however, the general meaning is not doubtful.] E.p. has: '. . . sees
itself, the affections of the soul feels [sic] such pain and affliction.'

[33] Job iii, 24.

[34] Job xxx, 17.

[35] H: 'never sleep.'

9. Deep is this warfare and this striving, for the peace which the soul hopes for will be very deep; and the spiritual pain is intimate and delicate,[36] for the love which it will possess will likewise be very intimate and refined. The more intimate and the more perfect the finished work is to be and to remain, the more intimate, perfect and pure must be the labour; the firmer the edifice, the harder the labour.[37] Wherefore, as Job says, the soul is fading within itself, and its vitals are being consumed without any hope.[38] Similarly, because in the state of perfection toward which it journeys by means of this purgative night the soul will attain to the possession and fruition of innumerable blessings, of gifts and virtues, both according to the substance of the soul and likewise[39] according to its faculties, it must needs see and feel itself withdrawn from them all and deprived of them all and be empty and poor without them;[40] and it must needs believe itself to be so far from them that it cannot persuade itself that it will ever reach them, but rather it must be convinced that all its good things are over. The words of Jeremias have a similar meaning in that passage already quoted, where he says: 'I have forgotten good things.'[41]

10. But let us now see the reason why this light of contemplation, which is so sweet and blessed to the soul that there is naught more desirable (for, as has been said above, it is the same wherewith the soul must be united and wherein it must find all the good things in the state of perfection that it desires), produces, when it assails the soul, these beginnings which are so painful and these effects which are so disagreeable, as we have here said.

11. This question is easy for us to answer, by explaining, as we have already done in part, that the cause of this is that, in contemplation and the Divine inflowing, there is naught that of itself can cause affliction, but that they rather cause

[36] E.p. adds: 'and refined.'
[37] Some MSS. omit the words 'the labour,' but the meaning is evidently the same.
[38] Job xxx, 16.
[39] E.p. omits 'likewise.'
[40] E.p. omits: 'and be empty . . . them.'
[41] Lamentations iii, 17.

great sweetness and delight, as we shall say hereafter.[42] The cause is rather the weakness and imperfection from which the soul then suffers, and the dispositions which it has in itself and which make it unfit for the reception of them. Wherefore, when[43] the said Divine light assails the soul, it must needs cause it to suffer after the manner aforesaid.

CHAPTER X

Explains this purgation fully by a comparison.[1]

FOR the greater clearness of what has been said, and of what has still to be said, it is well to observe at this point that this purgative and loving knowledge or Divine light whereof we here speak acts upon the soul which it is purging and preparing for perfect union with it in the same way as fire acts upon a log of wood in order to transform it into itself; for material fire, acting upon wood, first of all begins to dry it,[2] by driving out its moisture and causing it to shed the water which it contains within itself. Then it begins to make it black, dark and unsightly, and even to give forth a bad odour,[3] and, as it dries it little by little, it brings out and drives away all the dark and unsightly accidents which are contrary to the nature of fire. And, finally, it begins to kindle it externally and give it heat, and at last transforms it into itself and makes it as beautiful as fire. In this respect, the wood has neither passivity nor activity of its own,[4] save for its weight, which is greater, and its substance, which is denser, than that of fire, for it has in itself[5] the properties and activities of fire. Thus it is dry and it dries; it is hot and heats; it is bright and

[42] So Bz., C, H, Mtr. A, B, M: 'as was [*sic*] afterwards given it.' E.p.: 'as will afterwards be given it.' V: 'as was said before.'
[43] E.p. 'unfit [*lit.*, 'contrary': this also applies to our text] for the reception of that sweetness. And thus, when,' etc.
[1] So e.p. The Codices have no title.
[2] E.p.: 'to dry it up.'
[3] E.p. omits: 'and . . . odour.'
[4] E.p. has 'proper to wood' for 'of its own.'
[5] E.p.: 'which is less subtle than that of fire; it has in itself.'

gives brightness; and it is much less heavy than before. All these properties and effects are caused in it by the fire.

2. In this same way we have to philosophize with respect to this Divine fire of contemplative love, which, before it unites and transforms the soul in itself, first purges it of all its contrary accidents. It drives out its unsightliness, and makes it black and dark, so that it seems worse than before and more unsightly and abominable than it was wont to be.[6] For this Divine purgation is removing[7] all the evil and vicious humours which the soul has never perceived because they have been so deeply rooted and grounded in it; it has never realized, in fact, that it has had so much evil within itself. But now that they are to be driven forth and annihilated, these humours reveal themselves, and become visible to the soul because it is so brightly illumined by this dark light of Divine contemplation (although it is no worse than before, either in itself or in relation to God); and, as it sees in itself that which it saw not before, it is clear to it that not only is it unfit to be seen by God, but deserves His abhorrence, and that He does indeed abhor it. By this comparison[8] we can now understand many things concerning what we are saying and purpose to say.

3. First, we can understand how the very light and the loving wisdom which are to be united with the soul and to transform it are the same that at the beginning purge and prepare it: even as the very fire which transforms the log of wood into itself, and makes it part of itself, is that which at the first was preparing it for that same purpose.

4. Secondly, we shall be able to see how these afflictions are not felt by the soul as coming from the said Wisdom, since, as the Wise Man says, all good things together come to the soul with her.[9] They are felt as coming from the weakness and imperfection which belong to the soul; without such purgation, the soul cannot receive its Divine light, sweetness and delight, even as the log of wood, when the fire acts

[6] E.p. omits: 'and more . . . to be.'
[7] V: 'is consuming and removing.'
[8] Bz., H, V erroneously read: 'By this contemplation.'
[9] Wisdom vii, 11.

upon it, cannot immediately be transformed until it be made ready; wherefore the soul is greatly afflicted.[10] This statement is fully supported by the Preacher, where he describes all that he suffered in order that he might attain to union with wisdom and to the fruition of it, saying thus: 'My soul hath wrestled with her and my bowels were moved in acquiring her; therefore it shall possess[11] a good possession.'[12]

5. Thirdly, we can learn here incidentally in what manner souls are afflicted in purgatory. For the fire would have no power over them, even though they came into contact with it, if they had no imperfections for which to suffer.[13] These are the material upon which the fire of purgatory seizes; when that material is consumed there is naught else that can burn. So here, when the imperfections are consumed, the affliction of the soul ceases and its fruition remains.[14]

6. The fourth thing that we shall learn here is the manner wherein the soul, as it becomes purged and purified by means of this fire of love, becomes ever more enkindled in love,[15] just as the wood grows hotter in proportion as it becomes the better prepared by the fire. This enkindling of love, however, is not always felt by the soul, but only at times when contemplation assails it less vehemently, for then it has occasion to see, and even to enjoy, the work which is being wrought in it, and which is then revealed to it. For it seems that the worker takes his hand from the work, and draws the iron out of the furnace, in order that something of the work which is being done may be seen; and then there is occasion for the soul to observe in itself the good which it saw not while the work was going on. In the same way, when the flame ceases to attack the wood, it is possible to see how much of it has been enkindled.

[10] E.p.: 'wherefore the soul suffers greatly.'
[11] A, B: 'therefore shall I acquire.'
[12] Ecclesiasticus li, 28–9 [A.V., li, 19–21].
[13] E.p.: 'would have no power over them, if they were completely made ready to reign and be united with God in glory and had no faults for which to suffer.'
[14] E.p. adds: 'of the kind that in this life is possible.'
[15] E.p.: 'enkindled therein.'

7. Fifthly, we shall also learn from this comparison what has been said above—namely, how true it is that after each of these periods of relief the soul suffers once again, more intensely and keenly than before. For, after that revelation just referred to has been made, and after[16] the more outward imperfections of the soul have been purified, the fire of love once again attacks that which has yet to be consumed and purified more inwardly. The suffering of the soul now becomes more intimate, subtle and spiritual, in proportion as the fire refines away the finer,[17] more intimate and more spiritual imperfections, and those which are most deeply rooted in its inmost parts. And it is here just as with the wood, upon which the fire, when it begins to penetrate it more deeply, acts with more force and vehemence[18] in preparing its most inward part to possess it.

8.[19] Sixthly, we shall likewise learn here the reason why it seems to the soul that all its good is over, and that it is full of evil, since naught comes to it at this time but bitterness; it is like the burning[20] wood, which is touched by no air nor by aught else than by consuming fire. But, when there occur other periods of relief like the first, the rejoicing of the soul will be more interior because the purification has been more interior also.

9. Seventhly,[21] we shall learn that, although the soul has the most ample[22] joy at these periods (so much so that, as we said, it sometimes thinks that its trials[23] can never return again, although it is certain that[24] they will return quickly), it cannot fail to realize, if it is aware (and at times it is made aware) of a root of imperfection which remains, that its joy is incom-

---

[16] E.p.: 'and when at last.'
[17] [Lit., 'more delicate.']
[18] [Lit., 'fury.']
[19] This paragraph is only found in the Codices.
[20] Several Codices omit 'burning.'
[21] E.p.: 'Sixthly.'
[22] E.p.: 'intense.'
[23] E.p. clarifies the sense of this passage by substituting for 'they' of the MSS., 'the trials.'
[24] Thus e.p. The other authorities have: 'yet when' [probably in the sense, however, of 'nevertheless,' as in our text].

plete, because a new assault seems to be threatening it;[25] when this is so, the trial returns quickly. Finally, that which still remains to be purged and enlightened most inwardly cannot well be concealed from the soul in view of its experience of its former purification;[26] even as also in the wood it is the most inward part that remains longest unkindled,[27] and the difference between it and that which has already been purged is clearly perceptible; and, when this purification once more assails it most inwardly, it is no wonder if it seems to the soul once more that all its good is gone, and that it never expects to experience it again, for, now that it has been plunged into these most inward sufferings, all good coming from without is over.[28]

10. Keeping this comparison, then, before our eyes, together with what has already been said upon the first line of the first stanza concerning this dark night and its terrible properties, it will be well to leave these sad experiences of the soul and to begin to speak of the fruit of its tears and their blessed properties, whereof the soul begins to sing from this second line:

Kindled in love[29] with yearnings.

[25] [The sudden change of metaphor is the author's. The 'assault' is, of course, the renewed growth of the 'root.']

[26] [*Lit.*, '. . . from the soul, with regard to that which has already been purified.']

[27] [*Lit.*, 'not enlightened': the word is the same as that used just above.]

[28] [The word translated 'over' is rendered 'gone' just above.] So A, B, M. [P. Silverio reads, with] Bz., C, H, Mtr., V: 'blinded' [i.e., 'is shut out from it']. E.p.: 'is hidden from it.'

[29] [*Lit.*, 'in loves'; and so throughout the exposition of this line.]

CHAPTER XI

Begins to explain the second line of the first stanza. Describes how, as the fruit of these rigorous constraints, the soul finds itself with the vehement passion of Divine love.[1]

IN this line the soul describes the fire of love which, as we have said, like the material fire acting upon the wood, begins to take hold upon the soul in this night of painful contemplation. This enkindling now described, although in a certain way it resembles that which we described above as coming to pass in the sensual part of the soul, is in some ways as different from that other as is the soul from the body, or the spiritual part from the sensual. For this present kind is an enkindling of spiritual love in the soul, which, in the midst of these dark confines, feels itself to be keenly and sharply wounded in strong Divine love, and to have a certain realization and foretaste of God, although it understands nothing definitely, for, as we say, the understanding is in darkness.

2. The spirit feels itself here to be deeply and passionately in love, for this spiritual enkindling produces the passion of love. And, inasmuch as this love is infused, it is passive rather than active,[2] and thus it begets in the soul a strong passion of love. This love has in it something of union with God, and thus to some degree partakes of its properties, which are actions of God rather than of the soul, these being subdued within it passively. What the soul does here is to give its consent; the warmth and strength[3] and temper and passion of love—or enkindling, as the soul here calls it—belong[4] only to the love of God, which enters increasingly into union with it. This love finds in the soul more occasion and preparation to unite itself with it and to wound it, according as all the

---

[1] So e.p. The Codices make no division here.

[2] E.p.: '. . . is infused, the soul here concurs rather with its passive aspect.'

[3] E.p.: 'which are more especially actions of God received in the soul than of the soul itself, the soul giving them its simple and loving consent. Yet the warmth and strength,' etc.

[4] [*Lit.*, 'cling,' 'adhere.']

soul's desires are the more recollected,[5] and are the more withdrawn from and disabled for the enjoyment of aught either in Heaven or in earth.

3. This takes place to a great extent, as has already been said, in this dark purgation, for God has so weaned all the inclinations[6] and caused them to be so recollected[7] that they cannot find pleasure in anything they may wish. All this is done by God to the end that, when He withdraws them and recollects them in Himself, the soul may have more strength and fitness to receive this strong union of love of God, which He is now beginning to give it through this purgative way, wherein the soul must love with great strength and with all its desires and powers both of spirit and of sense; which could not be if they were dispersed in the enjoyment of aught else. For this reason David said to God, to the end that he might receive the strength of the love of this union with God: 'I will keep my strength for Thee;'[8] that is, I will keep the entire capacity and all the desires and energies of my faculties, nor will I employ their operation or pleasure in aught else than Thyself.

4. In this way it can be realized in some measure how great and how strong may be this enkindling of love in the spirit, wherein God keeps in recollection all the energies, faculties and desires of the soul, both of spirit and of sense, so that all this harmony may employ its energies and virtues in this love, and may thus attain to a true fulfilment of the first commandment, which sets aside nothing pertaining to man nor excludes from this love anything that is his, but says: 'Thou shalt love thy God with all thy heart and with all thy mind, with all thy soul and with all thy strength.'[9]

5. When all the desires and energies of the soul, then, have been recollected in this enkindling of love, and when the soul itself has been touched and wounded in them all, and has

[5] [Lit., 'shut up.']

[6] A, B, M have 'unbound' for 'weaned.' E.p. reads: 'for God has so weaned all the faculties.'

[7] [Here, and below, the original has recogidos, the word normally translated 'recollected.']

[8] Psalm lviii, 10 [A.V., lix, 9].

[9] Deuteronomy vi, 5.

been inspired with passion, what shall we understand the movements and digressions[10] of all these energies and desires to be, if they find themselves enkindled and wounded with strong love and without the possession and satisfaction thereof, in darkness and doubt? They will doubtless be suffering hunger, like the dogs of which David speaks as running about the city[11]; finding no satisfaction in this love, they keep howling and groaning. For the touch[12] of this love and Divine fire dries up the spirit and enkindles its desires,[13] in order to satisfy its thirst for this Divine love, so much so that it turns upon itself a thousand times and desires God in a thousand ways and manners, with the eagerness and desire of the appetite. This is very well explained by David in a psalm, where he says: 'My soul thirsted for Thee: in how many manners does my soul long for Thee!'[14]—that is, in desires. And another version reads: 'My soul thirsted for Thee, my soul is lost (*or* perishes) for Thee.'

6. It is for this reason that the soul says in this line that it was 'kindled in love with yearnings.'[15] For in all the things and thoughts that it revolves within itself, and in all the affairs and matters that present themselves to it, it loves in many ways, and also desires and suffers in the desire in many ways, at all times and in all places, finding rest in naught, and feeling this yearning in its enkindled wound,[16] even as the prophet Job declares, saying: 'As the hart[17] desireth the shadow,

[10] E.p.: 'and affections.'

[11] Psalm lviii, 15–16 [A.V., lix, 14–15].

[12] E.p.: '. . . and without satisfaction thereof, in darkness thereof and doubt? Suffering greater hunger, doubtless, as they have greater experience of God. For the touch.'

[13] E.p.: 'its affections.'

[14] Psalm lxii, 2 [A.V., lxiii, 1].

[15] [*Lit.*, as in the verses, 'in loves.'] Bz. adds: 'and says not "kindled in love with yearning."' H has: 'and says not "kindled in love and with yearning."'

[16] Thus the Codices. E.p. has: 'feeling this yearning enkindled and wounded.'

[17] [For *ciervo*, hart, read *siervo*, servant, and we have the correct quotation from Scripture. The change, however, was evidently made by the Saint knowingly. In P. Gerardo's edition, the Latin text, with *cervus*, precedes the Spanish translation, with *ciervo*.]

and as the hireling desireth the end of his work, so I also had vain months and numbered to myself wearisome and laborious nights. If I lie down to sleep, I shall say: "When shall I arise?" And then I shall await the evening and shall be full of sorrows even until the darkness of night.'[18] Everything becomes cramping to this soul: it cannot live[19] within itself; it cannot live either in Heaven or on earth; and it is filled with griefs until the darkness comes to which Job here refers, speaking spiritually and in the sense of our interpretation. What the soul here endures is affliction[20] and suffering without the consolation of a certain hope of any light and spiritual good. Wherefore the yearning and the grief of this soul in this enkindling of love are greater because it is multiplied in two ways: first, by the spiritual darkness wherein it finds itself, which afflicts it with its doubts and misgivings; and then by the love of God, which enkindles and stimulates it, and, with its loving wound, causes it a wondrous fear.[21] These two kinds of suffering at such a season are well described by Isaias, where he says: 'My soul desired Thee in the night'[22]— that is, in misery.

7. This is one kind of suffering which proceeds from this dark night; but, he goes on to say, with my spirit, in my bowels, until the morning, I will watch for Thee. And this is the second way of grieving in desire and yearning which comes from love in the bowels of the spirit, which are the spiritual affections. But in the midst of these dark and loving afflictions the soul feels within itself a certain companionship and strength, which bears it company and so greatly strengthens it that, if this burden of grievous darkness be taken away, it often feels itself to be alone, empty and weak. The cause of this is that, as the strength and efficacy of the soul were derived and communicated passively from the dark

[18] Job vii, 2-4.
[19] [No *cabe*: lit., 'it cannot be contained,' 'there is no room for it.']
[20] B, H, M: 'is expectation.'
[21] *Atemoriza* [evidently having puzzled the editor] is changed in e.p. into *atiza* ['stirs up'—the word used for poking the fire. I cannot think that the emendation, which repeats the idea of *estimula* above and finds no support in any MS., is worth adopting].
[22] Isaias xxvi, 9.

fire of love which assailed it, it follows that, when that fire ceases to assail it, the darkness and power and heat of love cease in the soul.[23]

CHAPTER XII

Shows how this horrible night is purgatory, and how in it the Divine wisdom illumines men on earth with the same illumination that purges and illumines the angels in Heaven.[1]

FROM what has been said we shall be able to see how this dark night of loving fire, as it purges in the darkness, so also in the darkness enkindles the soul. We shall likewise be able to see that, even as spirits[2] are purged in the next life with dark material fire, so in this life they are purged and cleansed with the dark spiritual fire of love. The difference is that in the next life they are cleansed with fire, while here below they are cleansed and illumined with love only. It was this love that David entreated, when he said: *Cor mundum crea in me, Deus*, etc.[3] For cleanness of heart is nothing less than the love and grace of God. For the clean of heart are called by our Saviour 'blessed'; which is as if He had called them 'enkindled with love',[4] since blessedness is given by nothing less than love.

2. And Jeremias well shows how the soul is purged when it is illumined with this fire of loving wisdom (for God never grants mystical wisdom without love, since love itself infuses it), where he says: 'He hath sent fire into my bones, and hath taught me.'[5] And David says that the wisdom of God is silver tried in fire[6]—that is, in purgative fire of love. For this dark contemplation infuses into the soul love and wisdom

---

[23] H reads only: 'the darkness ceases.'

[1] Chapter-heading and title are from e.p. The Codices make no division here.

[2] A, B: 'even as sins.' E.p.: 'even as the predestinate.'

[3] Psalm l, 12 [A.V., li, 10].

[4] [*Lit.*, 'enamoured.']

[5] Lamentations i, 13.

[6] Psalm xi, 7 [A.V., xii, 6].

jointly, to each one according to his capacity and need, enlightening the soul and purging it, in the words of the Wise Man, from its ignorances, as he said was done to himself.

3. From this we shall also infer that the very wisdom of God which purges these souls and illumines them[7] purges the angels from their ignorances, giving them knowledge, enlightening them as to that which they knew not,[8] and flowing down from God through the first hierarchies even to the last, and thence to men.[9] All the works, therefore, which are done by the angels, and all their inspirations, are said in the Scriptures, with truth and propriety, to be the work of God and of themselves; for ordinarily these inspirations come through the angels, and they receive them likewise one from another without any delay—as quickly as a ray of sunshine is communicated through many windows arranged in order. For although it is true that the sun's ray itself passes through them all, still each one passes it on and infuses it into the next, in a modified form, according to the nature of the glass, and with rather more or rather less power and brightness, according as it is nearer to the sun or farther from it.

4. Hence it follows that, the nearer to God are the higher spirits and the lower,[10] the more completely are they purged and enlightened with more general purification; and that the lowest of them will receive this illumination[11] very much less powerfully and more remotely. Hence it follows that man, who is the lowest of all those to whom this loving contemplation flows down continually from God, will, when God desires to give it him, receive it perforce after his own manner in a very limited way and with great pain.[12] For, when the

[7] The Codices omit the words 'purges . . . them', which are supplied by e.p.

[8] E.p. omits: 'giving . . . knew not.'

[9] The Schoolmen frequently assert that the lower angels are purged and illumined by the higher. Cf. St. Thomas, Summa, I, q. 106, a. 1, ad. 1.

[10] So e.p. The MSS. have: 'and those below.'

[11] E.p.: 'this enlightenment.'

[12] E.p. modifies thus: 'Hence it follows that, since man is lower than the angels, when God will give him this contemplation, he will perforce receive it after his manner, in a more limited way and with greater pain.'

light of God illumines an angel, it enlightens him and enkindles[13] him in love, since, being pure spirit, he is prepared
for that infusion. But, when it illumines man, who is impure
and weak, it illumines him, as has been said above, according
to his nature. It plunges him into darkness and causes him
affliction and distress, as does the sun to the eye that is weak;[14]
it enkindles him[15] with passionate yet afflictive love, until he
be spiritualized and refined by this same fire of love; and it
purifies him until he can receive with sweetness the union[16]
of this loving infusion after the manner of the angels, being
now purged, as by the help of the Lord we shall explain later.[17]
But meanwhile he receives this contemplation and loving
knowledge in the constraint and yearning of love of which
we are here speaking.

5. This enkindling and yearning of love are not always perceived by the soul. For in the beginning, when this spiritual
purgation commences, all this Divine fire is used in drying
up and making ready the wood (which is the soul) rather
than in giving it heat. But, as time goes on,[18] the fire begins
to give heat to the soul, and the soul then very commonly
feels this enkindling and heat of love. Further, as the understanding is being more and more purged by means of this
darkness, it sometimes comes to pass that this mystical and
loving theology, as well as enkindling the will, strikes and
illumines the other faculty also—that of the understanding—
with a certain Divine light and knowledge, so delectably and
delicately[19] that it aids the will to conceive a marvellous
fervour, and, without any action of its own,[20] there burns in
it this Divine fire of love, in living flames, so that it now
appears to the soul a living fire by reason of the living under-

---

[13] [Lit., 'and softens.']

[14] [More literally, 'is sick.'] So most MSS. and e.p. Bz.: 'impure
and sick.' H: 'bleared and sick.'

[15] A, e.p.: 'it enlightens him.'

[16] A, B, M: 'the infusion.'

[17] E.p. adds: 'For there are souls who in this life have received
more perfect illumination than the angels.'

[18] E.p. omits: 'as time goes on.'

[19] E.p.: 'and divinely.'

[20] E.p. omits: 'without . . . its own.'

standing which is given to it. It is of this that David speaks
in a Psalm, saying: 'My heart grew hot within me, and, as
I meditated, a certain fire was enkindled.'[21]

6. This enkindling of love, which accompanies the union
of these two faculties, the understanding and the will, which
are here united,[22] is for the soul a thing of great richness and
delight; for it is a certain touch of the Divinity and is already
the beginning[23] of the perfection of the union of love for
which it hopes. Now the soul attains not to this touch of so
sublime a sense and love of God, save when it has passed
through many trials and a great part of its purgation. But for
other touches which are much lower than these, and which
are of ordinary occurrence, so much purgation is not needful.

7.[24] From what we have said it may here be inferred how
in these spiritual blessings, which are passively infused by God
into the soul, the will may very well love even though the
understanding understand not; and similarly the understanding may understand and the will love not. For, since this dark
night of contemplation consists of Divine light and love, just
as fire contains light and heat, it is not unbefitting that, when
this loving light is communicated, it should strike the will at
times more effectively by enkindling it with love and leaving
the understanding in darkness instead of striking it with light;
and, at other times, by enlightening it with light, and giving
it understanding, but leaving the will in aridity (as it is also
true that the heat of the fire can be received without the
light being seen, and also the light of it can be seen without
the reception of heat); and this is wrought by the Lord, Who
infuses as He wills.[25]

[21] Psalm xxxviii, 4 [A.V., xxxix, 3].

[22] E.p. omits: 'which are here united.'

[23] [Lit., 'the beginnings.' E.p.: 'for it is certain that in this darkness it already has the beginnings.'

[24] The whole of this paragraph is omitted in e.p.

[25] The Saint here treats a question often debated by philosophers
and mystics—that of love and knowledge. Cf. also Spiritual Canticle, Stanza XVII, and Living Flame, Stanza III. Philosophers
generally maintain that it is impossible to love without knowledge,
and equally so to love more of an object than what is known of it.
Mystics have, however, their own solutions of the philosophers' difficulty and the speculative Spanish mystics have much to say on the

CHAPTER XIII

Of other delectable effects which are wrought in the soul by this dark night of contemplation.[1]

THIS type of enkindling will explain to us certain of the delectable effects which this dark night of contemplation works in the soul. For at certain times, as we have just said, the soul becomes enlightened in the midst of all this darkness, and the light shines in the darkness;[2] this mystical intelligence flows down into the understanding and the will remains in dryness—I mean, without actual union of love, with a serenity[3] and simplicity which are so delicate and delectable to the sense of the soul that no name can be given to them. Thus the presence of God is felt, now after one manner, now after another.

2. Sometimes, too, as has been said, it wounds the will at the same time, and enkindles love sublimely, tenderly and strongly; for we have already said that at certain times these two faculties, the understanding and the will, are united, when, the more they see,[4] the more perfect and delicate is the purgation of the understanding. But, before this state is reached, it is more usual for the touch of the enkindling of love to be felt in the will than for the touch of intelligence[5] to be felt in the understanding.

3.[6] But one question arises here, which is this: Why, since these two faculties are being purged together, are the en-

---

matter. (Cf., for example, the *Médula Mística*, Trat. V, Chap. iv, and the *Escuela de Oración*, Trat. XII, Duda v.)

[1] So e.p. The Codices make no division.

[2] St. John i, 5.

[3] E.p.: 'this mystical intelligence flows directly into the understanding and the will to some extent partakes of it, with a serenity,' etc.

[4] E.p. omits these four words, which are found in A, M. B, Bz., C, H, Mtr., V have: 'the more they go.' P: 'the more this is so.' [P. Gerardo follows P, which certainly best agrees with the general sense of the passage.]

[5] E.p.: 'of perfect intelligence.'

[6] E.p. omits this paragraph.

kindling and the love of purgative contemplation at first more commonly felt in the will than the intelligence thereof is felt in the understanding? To this it may be answered that this passive love does not now directly strike the will, for the will is free, and this enkindling of love is a passion of love rather than the free act of the will; for this heat of love strikes the substance of the soul and thus moves the affections passively. And so this is called passion of love rather than a free act of the will, an act of the will being so called only in so far as it is free. But these passions and affections subdue the will, and therefore it is said that, if the soul conceives passion with a certain affection, the will conceives passion; and this is indeed so, for in this manner the will is taken captive and loses its liberty, according as the impetus and power of its passion carry it away. And therefore we can say that this enkindling of love is in the will—that is, it enkindles the desire of the will; and thus, as we say, this is called passion of love rather than the free work of the will. And, because the receptive passion of the understanding can receive intelligence only in a detached and passive way (and this is impossible without its having been purged), therefore until this happens the soul feels the touch of intelligence less frequently than that of the passion of love. For it is not necessary to this end that the will should be so completely purged with respect to the passions, since these very passions help it to feel impassioned love.

4. This enkindling and thirst of love, which in this case belongs to the spirit, is very different from that other which we described in writing of the night of sense. For, though the sense has also its part here, since it fails not to participate in the labour of the spirit, yet the source and the keenness of the thirst of love is felt in the superior part of the soul—that is, in the spirit. It feels, and understands what it feels and its lack of what it desires, in such a way that all its affliction of sense, although greater without comparison than in the first night of sense, is as naught to it, because it recognizes within itself the lack of a great good which can in no way be measured.[7]

[7] Bz., e.p.: 'be remedied.'

5. But here we must note that although, at the beginning, when this spiritual night commences, this enkindling of love is not felt, because this fire of love has not begun to take a hold,[8] God gives the soul, in place of it, an estimative love of Himself so great that, as we have said, the greatest sufferings and trials of which it is conscious in this night are the anguished thoughts that it[9] has lost God and the fears that He has abandoned it. And thus we may always say that from the very beginning of this night the soul is touched with yearnings of love, which is now that of estimation,[10] and now again, that of enkindling. And it is evident that the greatest suffering which it feels in these trials is this misgiving; for, if it could be certified at that time that all is not lost and over, but that what is happening to it is for the best—as it is —and that God is not wroth, it would care naught for all these afflictions, but would rejoice to know that God is making use of them for His good pleasure. For the love of estimation which it has for God is so great, even though it may not realize this and may be in darkness, that it would be glad,[11] not only to suffer in this way, but even to die many times over in order to give Him satisfaction. But when once the flame has enkindled the soul, it is wont to conceive, to-gether with the estimation that it already has for God, such power and energy, and such yearning for Him, when He communicates to it the heat of love, that, with great boldness, it disregards everything and ceases to pay respect to anything, such are the power and the inebriation of love and desire. It regards not what it does, for[12] it would do strange and unusual things in whatever way and manner may present themselves, if thereby its soul might find Him Whom it loves.

6. It was for this reason that Mary Magdalene, though as

[8] E.p.: 'has not acted.'

[9] [*Lit.*, 'the yearning to think of it.']

[10] [The word translated 'estimation' might also be rendered 'reverent love.' The 'love of estimation,' which has its seat in the understanding, is contrasted with the 'enkindling' or the 'love of desire,' which has its seat in the will. So elsewhere in this paragraph.]

[11] E.p.: 'it would be very glad,' etc.

[12] E.p. omits: 'such are the power . . . what it does, for.'

greatly concerned for her own appearance as she was aforetime, took no heed[13] of the multitude of men who were at the
feast,[14] whether they were of little or of great importance;
neither did she consider that it was not seemly, and that it
looked ill, to go and weep and shed tears among the guests,
provided that, without delaying an hour or waiting for another time and season, she could reach Him for love of Whom
her soul was already wounded and enkindled. And such is the
inebriating power and the boldness[15] of love, that, though she
knew her Beloved to be enclosed in the sepulchre by the
great sealed stone, and surrounded by soldiers who were
guarding Him lest His disciples should steal Him away,[16] she
allowed none of these things to impede her, but went before
daybreak with the ointments to anoint Him.

7. And finally, this inebriating power and yearning of love
caused her to ask one whom she believed to be a gardener and
to have stolen Him away from the sepulchre, to tell her, if he
had taken Him, where he had laid Him, that she might take
Him away;[17] considering not that such a question, according
to independent judgment and reason, was foolish;[18] for it was
evident that, if the other had stolen Him, he would not say so,
still less would he allow Him to be taken away. It is a characteristic of the power and vehemence of love that all things
seem possible to it, and it believes all men to be of the same
mind as itself. For it thinks that there is naught wherein one
may be employed, or which[19] one may seek, save that which
it seeks itself and that which it loves; and it believes that
there is naught else to be desired, and naught wherein it may
be employed, save that one thing, which is pursued by all.[20]
For this reason, when the Bride went out to seek her Beloved,

[13] E.p.: 'Mary Magdalene, noble as she was, took no heed.'
[14] E.p.: 'at the feast which was given at the house of the Pharisee.
as Saint Luke says.'
[15] H: 'and the superfluity.'
[16] St. John xx, 1 [St. Matthew xxvii, 62–6].
[17] St. John xx, 15.
[18] E.p.: 'was not prudent.'
[19] E.p.: 'or no other thing which.'
[20] E.p.: omits 'which . . . all.'

through streets and squares,[21] thinking that all others were
doing the same, she begged them that, if they found Him,
they would speak to Him and say[22] that she was pining for
love of Him.[23] Such was the power of the love of this Mary
that she thought that, if the gardener would tell her where
he had hidden Him, she would go and take Him away, however difficult it might be made for her.

8. Of this manner, then, are the yearnings of love whereof
this soul becomes conscious when it has made some progress
in this spiritual purgation. For it rises up by night (that is,
in this purgative darkness) according to the affections of the
will. And with the yearnings and vehemence of the lioness or
the she-bear going to seek her cubs when they have been taken
away from her and she finds them not, does this wounded
soul go forth to seek its God. For, being in darkness, it feels
itself to be without Him and to be dying of love for Him.
And this is that impatient love wherein the soul cannot long
subsist without gaining its desire or dying. Such was Rachel's
desire for children when she said to Jacob: 'Give me children,
else shall I die.'[24]

9. But we have now to see how it is that the soul which
feels itself so miserable and so unworthy of God, here[25] in this
purgative darkness, has nevertheless strength, and is sufficiently
bold and daring, to journey towards union with God. The
reason is that, as love continually gives it strength wherewith
it may love indeed, and as the property of love is to desire
to be united, joined and made equal and like to the object
of its love, that it may perfect itself in love's good things,
hence it comes to pass that, when this soul is not perfected
in love, through not having as yet attained to union, the
hunger and thirst that it has for that which it lacks (which
is union) and the strength set by love in the will which has
caused it to become impassioned, make it bold and daring
by reason of the enkindling of its will, although in its under-

---

[21] [*Lit.*, 'outskirts,' 'suburbs.']
[22] E.p.: 'they would say of her.'
[23] Canticles v, 8.
[24] Genesis xxx, 1.
[25] E.p. has 'as it feels itself' for 'here.'

standing, which is still dark and unenlightened,[26] it feels itself
to be unworthy and knows itself to be miserable.

10. I will not here omit to mention the reason why this
Divine light, which is always light to the soul, illumines it
not as soon as it strikes it, as it does afterwards, but causes it
the darkness and the trials of which we have spoken. Something has already been said concerning this, but the question
must now be answered directly. The darkness and the other
evils of which the soul is conscious when this Divine light
strikes it are not darkness or evils caused by this light, but
pertain to the soul itself, and the light illumines it so that it
may see them. Wherefore it does indeed receive light from
this Divine light; but the soul cannot see at first, by its aid,
anything beyond what is nearest to it, or rather, beyond what
is within it—namely, its darknesses or its miseries, which it
now sees through the mercy of God, and saw not aforetime,
because this supernatural light illumined it not. And this is
the reason why at first it is conscious of nothing beyond darkness and evil; after it has been purged, however, by means
of the knowledge and realization of these, it will have eyes to
see, by the guidance of this light, the blessings of the Divine
light; and, once all these darknesses and imperfections[27] have
been driven out from the soul, it seems[28] that the benefits and
the great blessings which the soul is gaining in this blessed
night of contemplation become clearer.[29]

11. From what has been said, it is clear that God grants
the soul in this state the favour of purging it and healing it
with this strong lye of bitter purgation, according to its
spiritual and its sensual part, of all the imperfect habits and
affections which it had within itself with respect to temporal
things and to natural, sensual[30] and spiritual things, its inward faculties being darkened, and voided of all these, its

[26] E.p. omits: 'and unenlightened.'

[27] Bz., H, Mtr., P have 'impressions.' The other authorities read
'imperfections.'

[28] E.p.: 'it will have eyes to be shown the blessings of this Divine
light, and once all these darknesses and these imperfections of the
soul are driven out and taken away, it seems,' etc.

[29] E.p.: 'become known.'

[30] H adds 'speculative.'

spiritual and sensual affections being constrained and dried up, and its natural energies being attenuated and weakened with respect to all this (a condition which it could never attain of itself, as we shall shortly say). In this way God makes it to die to all that is not naturally[31] God, so that, once it is stripped and denuded of its former skin, He may begin to clothe it anew. And thus its youth is renewed like the eagle's and it is clothed with the new man, which, as the Apostle says, is created according to God.[32] This is naught else but His illumination of the understanding with super-natural light, so that it is no more a human understanding but becomes Divine through union with the Divine. In the same way the will is informed[33] with Divine love, so that it is a will that is now no less than Divine, nor does it love otherwise than divinely, for it is made and united in one with the Divine will and love. So, too, is it with the mem-ory; and likewise the affections and desires are all changed and converted[34] divinely, according to God. And thus this soul will now be a soul of heaven, heavenly, and more Divine than human. All this, as we have been saying, and because of what[35] we have said, God continues to do and to work in the soul by means of this night, illumining and enkindling it divinely with yearnings for God alone and for naught else whatsoever. For which cause the soul then very justly and reasonably adds the third line to the song, which says:[36]

. . . oh, happy chance!—
I went forth without being observed.

[31] E.p. omits 'naturally.'
[32] Ephesians iv, 24.
[33] Mtr., V, e.p.: 'enkindled.'
[34] E.p. omits: 'and converted.'
[35] E.p.: 'as will have been clearly seen from what.'
[36] E.p.: '. . . to the song, which, with the other lines, we shall set down and explain in the chapter following.'

CHAPTER XIV

*Wherein are set down and explained the last three lines of
the first stanza.[1]*

THIS happy chance was the reason for which the soul speaks,
in the next lines, as follows:

I went forth without being observed,   My house being now at rest.

It takes the metaphor[2] from one who, in order the better to
accomplish something, leaves his house by night and in the
dark, when those that are in the house are now at rest, so
that none may hinder him. For this soul had to go forth to
perform a deed so heroic and so rare—namely to become
united with its Divine Beloved—and it had to leave its house,
because the Beloved is not found save alone and without, in
solitude. It was for this reason that the Bride desired to find
Him alone, saying: 'Who would give Thee to me, my brother,[3]
that I might find Thee alone, without, and that my love might
be communicated to Thee.'[4] It is needful for the enamoured
soul, in order to attain to its desired end, to do likewise,
going forth at night, when all the domestics in its house are
sleeping and at rest—that is, when the low operations, passions and desires of the soul (who are the people of the household) are, because it is night, sleeping and at rest. When
these are awake, they invariably hinder the soul from seeking
its good, since they are opposed to its going forth in freedom.
These are they of whom Our Saviour speaks in the Gospel,
saying that they are the enemies of man.[5] And thus it would
be meet that their operations and motions should be put to
sleep in this night, to the end that they may not hinder the

[1] Thus e.p.
[2] E.p. modifies thus: 'The happy chance whereof the soul sings
in the first of these three lines was the reason for which it says in
the two following . . . taking the metaphor,' etc.
[3] A, B, M have: 'my spouse, my brother.'
[4] Canticles viii, I.
[5] St. Matthew x, 36.

soul from attaining the supernatural blessings of the union
of love of God, for, while these are alive and active, this
cannot be.[6] For all their work and their natural[7] motions
hinder, rather than aid, the soul's reception of the spiritual
blessings of the union of love, inasmuch as all natural ability
is impotent with respect to the supernatural blessings that
God, by means of His own infusion, bestows upon the soul
passively, secretly and in silence. And thus it is needful that
all the faculties should receive this infusion, and that, in order
to receive it, they should remain passive,[8] and not interpose
their own base acts and vile inclinations.

2. It was a happy chance for this soul that on this night
God should put to sleep all the domestics in[9] its house—that
is, all the faculties, passions, affections and desires which live
in the soul, both sensually and spiritually. For thus it went
forth 'without being observed'—that is, without being hindered by these affections, etc., for they were put to sleep and
mortified in this night, in the darkness of which they were
left, that they might not notice or feel anything after their
own low and natural manner, and might thus be unable to
hinder the soul from going forth from itself and from the
house of its sensuality. And thus only could the soul attain[10]
to the spiritual union of perfect love of God.[11]

3. Oh, how happy a chance is this for the soul which can
free itself from the house of its sensuality! None can understand it, unless, as it seems to me, it be the soul that has
experienced it. For such a soul will see clearly how wretched
was the servitude in which it lay and to how many miseries it
was subject when it was at the mercy of its faculties and

---

[6] E.p.: 'this cannot be attained.'
[7] E.p. omits 'natural.'
[8] E.p. omits: 'and . . . passive.'
[9] E.p. has 'all the people of.'
[10] The verb 'could attain' is found in e.p. but, though necessary to
the sense, is missing from all the MSS.
[11] So the MSS. E.p. modifies and shortens: 'which live in the sensual and spiritual soul, that it might attain to the spiritual union of
perfect love of God "without being observed"—that is, without being hindered by them, because they were put to sleep and mortified
in that night, as has been said.'

desires, and will know how the life of the spirit is true liberty
and wealth, bringing with it inestimable blessings. Some of
these we shall point out, as we proceed, in the following
stanzas, wherein it will be seen more clearly what good reason
the soul has to sing of[12] the happy chance of its passage from
this dreadful night which has been described above.

CHAPTER XV

Sets down the second stanza and its exposition.[1]

**In darkness and secure, By the secret ladder, dis-
guised—oh, happy chance!
In darkness and concealment, My house being now
at rest.**

IN this stanza the soul still continues to sing of certain
properties of the darkness of this night, reiterating how great
is the happiness which came to it through them. It speaks of
them in replying to a certain tacit objection, saying that[2] it is
not to be supposed that, because in this night and darkness it
has passed through so many tempests of afflictions, doubts,
fears and horrors, as has been said, it has for that reason run
any risk of being lost. On the contrary, it says, in the darkness of this night it has gained itself. For in the night it has
freed itself and escaped subtly from its enemies, who were
continually hindering its progress. For in the darkness of the
night it changed its garments and disguised itself with three
liveries and colours which we shall describe hereafter; and
went forth by a very secret ladder, which none in the house
knew, the which ladder, as we shall observe likewise in the
proper place, is living faith. By this ladder the soul went forth
in such complete hiding and concealment, in order the better
to execute its purpose, that it could not fail to be in great
security; above all since in this purgative night the desires,

12 A, P, e.p.: 'to relate.'
    1 So e.p. The Codices have only: 'Stanza the Second.' A, B have
no heading.
    2 E.p.: 'pointing out that.'

affections and passions of the soul are put to sleep, mortified and quenched, which are they that, when they were awake and alive, consented not to this.[3]

The first line, then, runs thus:[4]

In darkness and secure.

CHAPTER XVI

Explains how, though in darkness, the soul walks securely.[1]

THE darkness which the soul here describes relates, as we have said, to the desires and faculties, sensual, interior and spiritual, for all these are darkened in this night as to their natural light, so that, being purged in this respect, they may be illumined with respect to the supernatural. For the spiritual and the sensual desires are put to sleep and mortified, so that they can experience[2] nothing, either Divine or human; the affections of the soul are oppressed and constrained, so that they can neither move nor find support in anything; the imagination is bound and can make no useful reflection; the memory is gone; the understanding is in darkness, unable to understand anything;[3] and hence the will likewise is arid and constrained and all the faculties are void and useless;[4] and in addition to all this a thick and heavy cloud is upon the soul, keeping it in affliction, and, as it were, far away from God.[5]

[3] Thus Bz, H, P. The other MSS. and e.p. have: 'they that, were they awake and alive, would not consent to this.'

[4] [*Lit.*, 'The line, then, continues, and says thus.' In fact, however, the author is returning to the first line of the stanza.]

[1] So e.p.

[2] [*Lit.*, 'taste.' E.p. adds 'delectably.']

[3] E.p. omits: 'unable to understand anything.'

[4] E.p. omits: 'and useless.'

[5] Some have considered this description exaggerated, but it must be borne in mind that all souls are not tested alike and the Saint is writing of those whom God has willed to raise to such sanctity that they drain the cup of bitterness to the dregs. We have already seen (Bk. I, chap. xiv, § 5) that 'all do not experience (this) after one manner . . . for (it) is meted out by the will of God, in conformity with the greater or the smaller degree of imperfection

It is in this kind of 'darkness' that the soul says here[6] it travelled 'securely.'

2. The reason for this has been clearly expounded; for ordinarily the soul never strays save through its desires or its tastes or its reflections or its understanding or its affections; for as a rule it has too much or too little of these, or they vary or go astray, and hence the soul becomes inclined to that which behoves it not. Wherefore, when all these operations and motions are hindered, it is clear that the soul is secure against being led astray by them; for it is free, not only from itself, but likewise from its other enemies, which are the world and the devil. For when the affections and operations of the soul are quenched, these enemies cannot make war upon it by any other means or in any other manner.

3. It follows from this that, the greater is the darkness wherein the soul journeys and the more completely is it voided of its natural operations, the greater is its security. For, as the Prophet says,[7] perdition comes to the soul from itself alone—that is, from its sensual and interior desires and operations;[8] and good, says God, comes from Me alone. Wherefore, when it is thus hindered from following the things that lead it into evil, there will then come to it forthwith the blessings of union with God in its desires and faculties, which in that union He will make Divine and celestial. Hence, at the time of this darkness, if the soul considers the matter, it will see very clearly how little its desire and its faculties are being diverted to things that are useless and harmful; and how secure it is[9] from vainglory and pride and presumption, vain and false rejoicing and many other things. It follows clearly, then, that, by walking in darkness, not only is the soul not lost, but it has even greatly gained, since it is here gaining the virtues.

---

which each soul has to purge away, (and) in conformity, likewise, with the degree of love of union to which God is pleased to raise it' (p. 89, above).

[6] E.p.: 'It is in this kind of darkness that it says.'

[7] Osee xiii, 9.

[8] E.p. adds: 'not harmonized.'

[9] E.p.: 'to things that are useless and vain; and that it is secure,' etc.

4. But there is a question which at once arises here—namely, since the things of God are of themselves profitable to the soul and bring it gain and security, why does God, in this night, darken the desires and faculties with respect to these good things likewise, in such a way that the soul can no more taste of them[10] or busy itself with them than with these other things, and indeed in some ways can do so less? The answer is that it is well for the soul to perform no operation touching spiritual things at that time and to have no pleasure in such things, because its faculties and desires are base, impure and wholly natural; and thus, although these faculties be given the desire and interest in things supernatural and Divine, they could not receive them save after a base and a natural manner, exactly in their own fashion.[11] For, as the philosopher says, whatsoever is received comes to him that receives it after the manner of the recipient. Wherefore, since these natural faculties have neither purity nor strength nor capacity to receive and taste things that are supernatural after the manner of those things, which manner is Divine, but can do so only after their own manner, which is human and base, as we have said, it is meet that its faculties be in darkness concerning these Divine things likewise.[12] Thus, being weaned and purged and annihilated in this respect first of all, they may lose that base and human[13] way of receiving and acting, and thus all these faculties and desires of the soul may come to be prepared and tempered in such a way as to be able to receive, feel and taste that which is Divine and supernatural[14] after a sublime and lofty manner, which is impossible if the old man die not first of all.

[10] B, e.p.: 'can no more enjoy them.'

[11] E.p. modifies: 'that it is meet at that time for its operation and pleasure to be void as touching spiritual things; for its faculties and desires are base and impure; and thus, even though these faculties should be given desire and interest in things supernatural and Divine, they could not receive them save after a base manner.'

[12] E.p.: '. . . which manner is Divine, but after their own manner; it is meet that [its faculties] be in darkness concerning these Divine things likewise, for perfect purgation.'

[13] E.p. omits: 'and human.'

[14] E.p. omits: 'and supernatural.'

5. Hence it follows that all spiritual things, if they come not from above and be not communicated by the Father of lights to human desire and free will (howsoever much a man may exercise his taste and faculties for God, and howsoever much it may seem to the faculties that they are experiencing these things), will not be experienced after a Divine and spiritual manner, but after a human and natural manner, just as other things are experienced, for spiritual blessings go not from man to God, but come from God to man.[15] With respect to this (if this were the proper place for it) we might here explain how there are many persons whose many tastes and affections and the operations of whose faculties are fixed upon God or upon spiritual things, and who may perhaps think that this is supernatural and spiritual, when it is perhaps no more than the most human[16] and natural desires[17] and actions. They regard these good things with the same disposition as they have for other things, by means of a certain natural facility which they possess for directing their desires and faculties to anything whatever.

6. If perchance we find[18] occasion elsewhere in this book, we shall treat of this, describing certain signs which indicate when the interior actions and motions of the soul, with respect to communion with God, are only natural, when they are spiritual, and when they are both natural and spiritual. It suffices for us here to know that, in order that the interior motions and acts of the soul may come to be moved by God divinely, they must first be darkened and put to sleep and hushed to rest naturally[19] as touching all their capacity and operation, until they have no more strength.

7. Therefore, O spiritual soul, when thou seest thy desire obscured, thy affections arid and constrained, and thy faculties

[15] E.p. modifies: 'howsoever much the taste and desire of man and his faculties with respect to God be exercised, and howsoever much it may seem to them that they experience Him, they experience Him not in this way divinely and perfectly.'

[16] E.p.: 'than very human.'

[17] A, B, M read 'trials' [aprietos] for 'desires' [apetitos].

[18] A, B, P, e.p.: 'we have.'

[19] A, e.p. [clarify the somewhat vague adverb by reading]: 'in that which is natural.'

bereft of their capacity for any interior exercise, be not afflicted by this, but rather consider it a great happiness, since
God is freeing thee from thyself and taking the matter from
thy hands. For with those hands, howsoever well they may
serve thee, thou wouldst never labour so effectively, so perfectly and so securely (because of their clumsiness and uncleanness) as now, when God takes thy hand and guides thee
in the darkness, as though thou wert blind, to an end and by
a way which thou knowest not. Nor couldst thou ever hope
to travel with the aid of thine own eyes and feet, howsoever
good thou be as a walker.

8. The reason, again, why the soul not only travels securely,
when it travels thus in the darkness, but also achieves even
greater gain and progress, is that usually, when the soul is
receiving fresh advantage and profit, this comes by a way
that it least understands—indeed, it quite commonly believes
that it is losing ground. For, as it has never experienced that
new feeling which drives it forth and[20] dazzles it and makes
it depart recklessly from its former way of life, it thinks itself
to be losing ground rather than gaining and progressing, since
it sees that it is losing with respect to that which it knew
and enjoyed, and is going by a way which it knows not and
wherein it finds no enjoyment. It is like the traveller, who,
in order to go to new and unknown lands,[21] takes new roads,
unknown and untried, and journeys unguided by his past
experience, but doubtingly and according to what others say.
It is clear that such a man could not reach new countries,
or add to his past experience, if he went not along new and
unknown roads and abandoned those which were known to
him.[22] Exactly so, one who is learning fresh details concerning
any office or art always proceeds in darkness, and receives
no guidance from his original knowledge, for if he left not
that behind he would get no farther nor make any progress;
and in the same way, when the soul is making most progress, it

[20] E.p. omits: 'drives it forth and.'
[21] M adds: 'and untried' and omits: 'takes . . . untried, and.'
[22] E.p. modifies: 'unknown and untried by the report of any other
person, and would clearly never reach new countries save by new and
unknown roads, abandoning those which were known to him.'

is travelling in darkness, knowing naught. Wherefore, since God, as we have said, is the Master and Guide of this blind soul, it may well and truly rejoice, once it has learned to understand this, and say: 'In darkness and secure.'

9. There is another reason why the soul has walked securely in this darkness, and this is because it has been suffering; for the road of suffering is more secure and even more profitable than that of fruition and action: first, because in suffering the strength of God is added to that of man, while in action and fruition the soul is practising its own weaknesses and imperfections; and second, because in suffering the soul continues to practise and acquire the virtues and become purer, wiser and more cautious.

10. But there is another and a more important reason why the soul now walks in darkness and securely;[23] this emanates from the dark light or wisdom aforementioned. For in such a way does this dark night of contemplation absorb and immerse the soul in itself, and so near does it bring the soul to God, that it protects and delivers it from all that is not God. For this soul is now, as it were, undergoing a cure, in order that it may regain its health—its health being God Himself. His Majesty restricts it to a diet and abstinence from all things, and takes away its appetite for them all. It is like a sick man, who, if he is respected by those in his house, is carefully tended so that he may be cured; the air is not allowed to touch him, nor may he even enjoy the light, nor must he hear footsteps, nor yet the noise of those in the house; and he is given food that is very delicate, and even that only in great moderation—food that is nourishing rather than delectable.

11. All these particularities (which are for the security and safekeeping of the soul) are caused by this dark contemplation, because it brings the soul nearer to God. For[24] the nearer the soul approaches Him, the blacker is the darkness which it feels and the deeper is the obscurity which comes through its weakness; just as, the nearer a man approaches the sun, the greater are the darkness and the affliction caused

[23] A, e.p.: 'now, walking in darkness, walks securely.'
[24] A, e.p.: 'For, in truth.'

him through the great splendour of the sun and through the weakness and impurity[25] of his eyes. In the same way, so immense is the spiritual light of God, and so greatly does it transcend our natural understanding, that the nearer we approach it, the more it blinds and darkens us. And this is the reason why, in Psalm xvii, David says that God made darkness His hiding-place and covering, and His tabernacle around Him dark water in the clouds of the air.[26] This dark water in the clouds of the air is dark contemplation and Divine wisdom in souls, as we are saying. They continue to feel it is a thing which is near Him, as the tabernacle wherein He dwells, when God brings them ever nearer to Himself. And thus, that which in God is supreme light and refulgence is to man blackest darkness, as Saint Paul says, according as David explains in the same Psalm, saying: 'Because of the brightness which is in His presence, passed clouds and cataracts'[27]—that is to say, over the natural understanding, the light whereof, as Isaias says in Chapter V: *Obtenebrata est in caligine ejus.*[28]

12. Oh, miserable is the fortune of our life, which is lived in such great peril and wherein it is so difficult to find the truth! For that which is most clear and true is to us most dark and doubtful; wherefore, though it is the thing that is most needful for us, we flee from it. And that which gives the greatest light and satisfaction to our eyes we embrace and pursue, though it be the worst thing for us, and make us fall at every step. In what peril and fear does man live, since the very natural light of his eyes by which he has to guide himself[29] is the first light that dazzles him and leads him astray on his road to God! And if he is to know with certainty by what road he travels, he must perforce keep his eyes closed and walk in darkness, that he may be secure from the enemies who inhabit his own house—that is, his senses and faculties.

---

[25] A, e.p. add: 'and defectiveness.'
[26] Psalm xvii, 12 [A.V., xviii, 11]. A alone gives the passage both in Latin and in Spanish.
[27] Psalm xvii, 13 [A.V., xviii, 12].
[28] Isaias v, 30.
[29] E.p.: 'wherewith he guides himself.'

13. Well hidden, then, and well protected is the soul in these dark waters, when it is close to God. For, as these waters serve as a tabernacle and dwelling-place for God Himself, they will serve the soul in the same way and for a perfect protection and security, though it remain in darkness, wherein, as we have said, it is hidden[30] and protected from itself, and from all evils[31] that come from creatures; for to such the words of David refer in another Psalm, where he says: 'Thou shalt hide them in the hiding-place of Thy face from the disturbance of men; Thou shalt protect them in Thy tabernacle from the contradiction of tongues.'[32] Herein we understand all kinds of protection; for to be hidden in the face of God from the disturbance of men is to be fortified with this dark contemplation against all the chances which may come upon the soul from men. And to be protected in His tabernacle from the contradiction of tongues is for the soul to be engulfed in these dark waters, which are the tabernacle of David whereof we have spoken. Wherefore, since the soul has all its desires and affections weaned and its faculties set in darkness, it is free from all imperfections which contradict the spirit, whether they come from its own flesh or from other creatures. Wherefore this soul may well say that it journeys 'in darkness and secure.'

14. There is likewise another reason, which is no less effectual than the last, by which we may understand how the soul journeys securely in darkness;[33] it is derived from the fortitude by which the soul is at once inspired in these obscure and afflictive dark waters of God. For after all, though the waters be dark, they are none the less waters, and therefore they cannot but refresh and fortify the soul in that which is most needful for it, although in darkness and with affliction. For the soul immediately perceives in itself a genuine determination and an effectual desire to do naught which it understands to be an offence to God, and to omit to do naught that seems to be for His service. For that

---

[30] E.p.: 'though in darkness, where it is hidden.'
[31] A, V, e.p.: 'and from all the other evils.'
[32] Psalm xxx, 21 [A.V., xxxi, 20].
[33] E.p.: 'journeys well, though in darkness.'

dark love cleaves to the soul, causing it a most watchful care and an inward solicitude concerning that which it must do, or must not do, for His sake, in order to please Him. It will consider and ask itself a thousand times if it has given Him cause to be offended; and all this it will do with much greater care and solicitude than before, as has already been said with respect to the yearnings of love. For here all the desires and energies and faculties of the soul are recollected from all things else, and its effort and strength are employed in pleasing its God alone.[34] After this manner the soul goes forth from itself and from all created things to the sweet and delectable union of love of God, 'In darkness and secure.'

By the secret ladder, disguised.

CHAPTER XVII

Explains how this dark contemplation is secret.[1]

THREE things have to be expounded with reference to three words contained in this present line. Two (namely, 'secret' and 'ladder') belong to the dark night of contemplation of which we are treating; the third (namely, 'disguised') belongs to the soul by reason of the manner wherein it conducts itself in this night.[2] As to the first, it must be known that in this line the soul describes this dark contemplation, by which it goes forth to the union of love, as a secret ladder, because of the two properties which belong to it—namely, its being secret and its being a ladder. We shall treat of each separately.[3]

2. First, it describes this dark contemplation as 'secret,' since, as we have indicated above, it is mystical theology,

---

[34] E.p.: '. . . of the soul, since they are recollected from all things else, employ their effort and strength in pleasing their God alone.'

[1] So e.p. The Codices make no division.

[2] E.p.: 'but the third, which is "disguised," touches the manner wherein the soul conducts itself in this night.'

[3] E.p. abbreviates: 'which belong to it, and which we shall proceed to expound.'

which theologians call secret wisdom,[4] and which, as Saint Thomas says, is communicated and infused into the soul through love.[5] This happens[6] secretly and in darkness, so as to be hidden from the work[7] of the understanding and of other faculties. Wherefore, inasmuch as the faculties afore-mentioned attain not to it, but the Holy Spirit infuses and orders it in the soul,[8] as says the Bride in the Songs, without either its knowledge or its understanding, it is called secret. And, in truth, not only does the soul not understand it, but there is none that does so, not even the devil; inasmuch as the Master Who teaches the soul is within it in its sub-stance, to which the devil may not attain, neither may nat-ural sense nor understanding.[9]

3. And it is not for this reason alone that it may be called secret, but likewise because of the effects which it produces in the soul. For it is secret not only in the darknesses and afflictions of purgation, when this wisdom of love[10] purges the soul, and the soul is unable to speak of it, but equally so afterwards in illumination, when this wisdom is commu-nicated to it most clearly. Even then it is still so secret that the soul cannot speak of it[11] and give it a name whereby it may be called; for, apart from the fact that the soul has no desire to speak of it, it can find no suitable way or manner or similitude by which it may be able to describe such lofty understanding and such delicate[12] spiritual feeling. And thus, even though the soul might have a great desire to express it and might find many ways in which to describe it, it would still be secret and remain undescribed.[13] For, as that inward wisdom is so simple, so general and so spiritual that it has

----

[4] H: 'mystical wisdom.'

[5] 'Propter hoc Gregorius (Hom. 14 in Ezech.) constituit vitam contemplativam in charitate Dei.' Cf. *Summa Theologica*, 2a, 2æ, q. 45, a. 2.

[6] E.p.: 'through love more especially. And this happens.'

[7] A, e.p.: 'from the natural work.'

[8] E.p. omits: 'and orders.' A, B, M read: 'infuses and adorns it.'

[9] E.p. omits: 'to which . . . understanding.'

[10] A, B, e.p.: 'this secret wisdom.'

[11] E.p.: 'cannot discern it.'

[12] E.p.: 'delicate and infused.'

[13] E.p.: 'it would ever remain secret.'

not entered into the understanding enwrapped or cloaked in any form or image subject to sense,[14] it follows that sense and imagination (as it has not entered through them nor has taken their form and colour) cannot account for it or imagine it, so as to say anything concerning it,[15] although the soul be clearly aware that it is experiencing and partaking of that rare and delectable wisdom. It is like one who sees something never seen before, whereof he has not even seen the like; although he might understand its nature and have experience of it, he would be unable to give it a name, or say what it is, however much he tried to do so, and this in spite of its being a thing which he had perceived with the senses. How much less, then, could he describe a thing that has not entered through the senses! For the language of God has this characteristic that, since it is very intimate and spiritual[16] in its relations with the soul, it transcends every sense and at once makes all harmony and capacity of the outward and inward senses to cease and be dumb.

4. For this we have both authorities and examples in the Divine Scripture. For the incapacity of man to speak of it and describe it in words was shown by Jeremias,[17] when, after God had spoken with him, he knew not what to say, save 'Ah, ah, ah!' This interior incapacity—that is, of the interior sense of the imagination—and also that of the exterior sense corresponding to it was also demonstrated in the case of Moses, when he stood before God in the bush;[18] not only did he say to God that after speaking with Him he knew not neither was able to speak, but also that not even (as is said in the Acts of the Apostles)[19] with the interior imagination did he dare to meditate, for it seemed to him that his imagination was very far away and was too dumb, not only to express any part of that which he understood concerning God, but even to have the capacity to receive aught therefrom. Wherefore, inas-

[14] E.p. adds: 'as sometimes happens.'
[15] E.p.: 'or imagine it, in such a manner as to be able to say anything well concerning it.'
[16] E.p.: 'that, when it is very intimate, infused and spiritual.'
[17] Jeremias i, 6.
[18] Exodus iv, 10 [cf. iii, 2].
[19] Acts vii, 32.

much as the wisdom of this contemplation is the language of God to the soul, addressed by pure spirit to pure spirit, naught that is less than spirit, such as the senses, can perceive it, and thus to them it is secret, and they know it not, neither can they say it,[20] nor do they desire to do so, because they see it not.[21]

5. We may deduce from this the reason why certain persons—good and fearful souls—who walk along this road and would like to give an account of their spiritual state to their director,[22] are neither able to do so nor know how. For the reason we have described,[23] they have a great repugnance in speaking of it,[24] especially when their contemplation is of the purer sort, so that the soul itself is hardly conscious of it. Such a person is only able to say that he is satisfied, tranquil and contented and that he is conscious of the presence of God, and that, as it seems to him, all is going well with him; but he cannot describe the state of his soul, nor can he say anything about it save in general terms like these. It is a different matter when the experiences of the soul are of a particular kind, such as visions, feelings, etc., which, being ordinarily received under some species wherein sense participates, can be described under that species, or by some other similitude. But this capacity for being described is not in the nature of pure contemplation, which is indescribable, as we have said,[25] for the which reason it is called secret.

6. And not only for that reason is it called secret, and is so, but likewise because this mystical knowledge has the property of hiding the soul within itself. For, besides performing its ordinary function, it sometimes absorbs the soul and engulfs

[20] [Or: 'and they know not how to say it nor are able to do so.']
[21] E.p. abbreviates: 'was very far away and dumb. And as the wisdom of this contemplation is the language of God to the soul, of [or 'from'] pure spirit, the senses, which are not this [i.e., 'pure spirit'], perceive it not, and thus it is secret to them, and they know it not, neither can they say it.'
[22] [Lit., 'to him that rules them.']
[23] E.p.: 'And thus.'
[24] A, B: 'Hence arises the great repugnance that they have in speaking of it.'
[25] E.p.: 'which can hardly be described.'

it in its secret abyss, in such a way that the soul clearly sees that it has been carried far away from every creature and has become most remote therefrom;[26] so that it considers itself as having been placed in a most profound and vast retreat, to which no human creature can attain, such as an immense desert, which nowhere has any boundary, a desert the more delectable, pleasant and lovely for its secrecy, vastness and solitude, wherein, the more the soul is raised up above all temporal creatures, the more deeply does it find itself hidden. And so greatly does this abyss of wisdom raise up and exalt the soul at this time, making it to penetrate the veins of the science of love, that it not only shows it how base are all properties of the creatures by comparison with this supreme knowledge and Divine feeling, but likewise it learns how base and defective, and, in some measure, how inapt, are all the terms and words which are used in this life to treat of Divine things, and how impossible it is,[27] in any natural way or manner, however learnedly and sublimely they may be spoken of, to be able to know and perceive them as they are, save by the illumination of this mystical theology. And thus, when by means of this illumination the soul discerns this truth, namely, that it cannot reach it, still less explain it, by common or human language, it rightly calls it secret.

7. This property of secrecy and superiority over natural capacity, which belongs to this Divine contemplation, belongs to it, not only because it is supernatural, but also inasmuch as it is a road that guides and leads the soul[28] to the perfections of union with God; which, as they are things unknown after a human manner, must be approached, after a human manner,[29] by unknowing and by Divine ignorance. For, speaking mystically, as we are speaking here, Divine things and perfections[30] are known and understood as they are, not

---

[26] [*Lit.*, 'that is set most far away and most remote from every creature.'] E.p. has 'most completely abandoned' for 'most far away.'

[27] E.p.: 'and how it is not possible.'

[28] E.p.: 'inasmuch as it is a guide that guides the soul.'

[29] E.p. omits: 'after a human manner.'

[30] E.p. has 'these things' and omits 'and perfections.'

when they are being sought after and practised,[31] but when they have been found and practised. To this purpose speaks the prophet Baruch concerning this Divine wisdom: 'There is none that can know her ways nor that can imagine her paths.'[32] Likewise the royal Prophet speaks in this manner concerning this road of the soul, when he says to God: 'Thy lightnings lighted and illumined the round earth; the earth was moved and trembled.[33] Thy way[34] is in the sea and Thy paths are in many waters; and Thy footsteps shall not be known.'[35]

8. All this, speaking spiritually, is to be understood in the sense wherein we are speaking. For the illumination of the round earth[36] by the lightnings[37] of God is the enlightenment which is produced by this Divine contemplation in the faculties of the soul; the moving and trembling of the earth is the painful purgation which is caused therein; and to say that the way and the road of God whereby the soul journeys to Him is in the sea, and His footprints are in many waters and for this reason shall not be known, is as much as to say that this road whereby the soul journeys to God is as secret and as hidden from the sense of the soul as the way of one that walks on the sea, whose paths and footprints are not known, is hidden from the sense of the body. The steps and footprints which God is imprinting upon the souls that He desires to bring near to Himself, and to make great in union with His Wisdom, have also this property, that they are not known. Wherefore in the Book of Job mention is made of this matter, in these words: 'Hast thou perchance known the paths of the

---

[31] E.p. omits: 'and practised.'

[32] Baruch iii, 31.

[33] P omits this passage and G omits an entire page here. Other MSS. have various words for that which is here rendered 'trembled' [but English has only the one word which fairly expresses them all].

[34] E.p.: 'Thy road.'

[35] Psalm lxxvi, 19–20 [A.V., lxxvii, 18–19].

[36] [Lit., 'of the roundness of the earth.']

[37] [coruscaciones.] A, P, e.p.: ilustraciones [the word translated 'lightnings' at the end of § 7; the singular is rendered 'enlightenment' in this present clause].

great clouds or the perfect knowledges?'[38] By this are understood the ways and roads whereby God continually exalts souls and perfects them in His Wisdom, which souls are here understood by the clouds. It follows, then, that this contemplation which is guiding the soul to God is secret wisdom.

CHAPTER XVIII

Explains how this secret wisdom is likewise a ladder.[1]

IT now remains[2] to consider the second point—namely, how this secret wisdom is likewise a ladder. With respect to this it must be known that we can call this secret contemplation a ladder for many reasons. In the first place, because, just as men mount by means of ladders and climb up to possessions and treasures and things that are in strong places, even so also, by means of this secret contemplation, without knowing how, the soul ascends and climbs up to a knowledge and possession of[3] the good things and treasures of Heaven. This is well expressed by the royal prophet David, when he says: 'Blessed is he that hath Thy favour and help, for such a man hath placed in his heart ascensions into the vale of tears in the place which he hath appointed;[4] for after this manner the Lord of the law shall give blessing, and they shall go from virtue to virtue as from step to step, and the God of gods shall be seen in Sion.'[5] This God is the treasure of the strong place of Sion, which is happiness.

2. We may also call it a ladder because, even as the ladder has those same steps in order that men may mount, it has them also that they may descend; even so is it likewise with this secret contemplation, for those same communications which it causes in the soul raise it up to God, yet humble it

---

[38] Job xxxvii, 16.
[1] So e.p. There is no division in the Codices.
[2] E.p.: 'It remains.'
[3] [*Lit.*, 'rises to scale, know and possess.']
[4] A: 'for such a man hath placed in his heart of sighs'; B: 'for such a man hath placed in his heart his sighs.'
[5] Psalm lxxxiii, 6 [A.V., lxxxiv, 7].

with respect to itself. For communications which are indeed of God have this property, that they humble the soul and at the same time exalt it. For, upon this road, to go down is to go up, and to go up, to go down, for he that humbles himself is exalted and he that exalts himself is humbled.[6] And besides the fact that the virtue of humility is greatness, for the exercise of the soul therein, God is wont to make it mount by this ladder so that it may descend, and to make it descend so that it may mount, that the words of the Wise Man may thus be fulfilled, namely: 'Before the soul is exalted, it is humbled; and before it is humbled, it is exalted.'[7]

3. Speaking now in a natural way,[8] the soul that desires to consider it will be able to see how on this road (we leave apart the spiritual aspect, of which the soul is not conscious) it has to suffer many ups and downs, and how the prosperity which it enjoys is followed immediately by certain storms and trials; so much so, that it appears to have been given that period of calm in order that it might be forewarned and strengthened against the poverty which has followed;[9] just as after misery and torment there come abundance and calm. It seems to the soul as if, before celebrating that festival, it has first been made to keep that vigil. This is the ordinary course and proceeding of the state of contemplation until the soul arrives at the state of quietness; it never remains in the same state for long together, but is ascending and descending continually.

4. The reason for this is that, as the state of perfection, which consists in the perfect love of God and contempt for self, cannot exist unless it have these two parts, which are the knowledge of God and of oneself, the soul has of necessity to be practised first in the one and then in the other, now being given to taste of the one—that is, exaltation—and now being made to experience the other—that is, humiliation—

[6] St. Luke xiv, 11.

[7] Proverbs xviii, 12.

[8] So H. A, B, M read [*hablando ahora manualmente*, which in its context I take to mean]: 'Speaking now in a homely way'; Bz., Mtr., V: 'in a somewhat homely way.' E.p. has: 'Likewise, according to this quality of a ladder, the soul,' etc.

[9] E.p.: 'against its present hardships.'

until it has acquired perfect habits; and then this ascending and descending will cease, since the soul will have attained to God and become united with Him, which comes to pass at the summit of this ladder, for the ladder rests and leans upon Him. For this ladder of contemplation, which, as we have said, comes down from God, is prefigured by that ladder which Jacob saw as he slept, whereon angels were ascending and descending, from God to man, and from man to God, Who Himself was leaning upon the end of the ladder.[10] All this, says Divine Scripture, took place by night, when Jacob slept, in order to express how secret is this road and ascent to God, and how different from that of man's knowledge. This is very evident, since ordinarily that which is of the greatest profit in it—namely, to be ever losing oneself and becoming as nothing[11]—is considered the worst thing possible; and that which is of least worth, which is for a soul to find consolation and sweetness (wherein it ordinarily loses rather than gains), is considered best.

5. But, speaking now somewhat more substantially and properly of this ladder of secret contemplation, we shall observe that the principal characteristic of contemplation, on account of which it is here called a ladder, is that it is the science of love. This, as we have said,[12] is an infused and loving knowledge of God, which enlightens the soul and at the same time enkindles it with love, until it is raised up step by step, even unto God its Creator. For it is love alone that unites and joins the soul with God. To the end that this may be seen more clearly, we shall here indicate the steps of this Divine ladder one by one, pointing out briefly the marks and effects of each, so that the soul may conjecture hereby on which of them it is standing. We shall therefore distinguish them by their effects, as do Saint Bernard and Saint Thomas,[13] for

[10] Genesis xxviii, 12.

[11] [Lit., 'and annihilating oneself.']

[12] E.p. omits: 'as we have said.'

[13] 'Ut dicit Bernardus, Magna res est amor, sed sunt in eo gradus. Loquendo ergo aliquantulum magis moraliter quam realiter, decem amoris gradus distinguere possumus' (D. Thom., De dilectione Dei et proximi, cap. xxvii. Cf. Opusc. LXI of the edition of Venice, 1595).

to know them in themselves is not possible after a natural manner, inasmuch as this ladder of love is, as we have said, so secret that God alone is He that measures and weighs it.

CHAPTER XIX

Begins to explain the ten steps[1] of the mystic ladder of Divine love, according to Saint Bernard and Saint Thomas. The first five are here treated.[2]

WE observe, then, that the steps of this ladder of love by which the soul mounts, one by one, to God, are ten. The first step of love causes the soul to languish, and this to its advantage. The Bride is speaking from this step of love when she says: 'I adjure you, daughters of Jerusalem, that, if ye find my Beloved, ye tell Him that I am sick with love.'[3] This sickness, however, is not unto death, but for the glory of God, for in this sickness the soul[4] swoons as to sin and as to all things that are not God, for the sake of God Himself, even as David testifies, saying: 'My soul hath swooned away'[5] —that is, with respect to all things, for Thy salvation. For just as a sick man first of all loses his appetite and taste for all food, and his colour changes, so likewise in this degree of love the soul loses its taste and desire for all things and changes its colour and the other accidentals of its past life,[6] like one in love. The soul falls not into this sickness if excess of heat be not communicated to it from above,[7] even as is expressed in that verse of David which says: *Pluviam voluntariam segregabis, Deus, hæreditati tuæ, et infirmata est,*[8]

[1] [The word translated 'step' may also (and often more elegantly) be rendered 'degree.' The same word is kept, however, throughout the translation of this chapter except where noted below.]

[2] So e.p. The Codices make no division.

[3] Canticles v, 8.

[4] E.p.: 'for herein the soul.'

[5] Psalm cxlii, 7 [A.V., cxliii, 7].

[6] E.p. omits: 'and the . . . life.'

[7] E.p. adds: 'which is here the mystic fever.'

[8] Psalm lxvii, 10 [A.V., lxviii, 9]. The Latin text is found in all the Codices except C, G, P.

etc. This sickness and swooning to all things, which is the beginning and the first step on the road to God, we clearly described above, when we were speaking of the annihilation wherein the soul finds itself when it begins to climb[9] this ladder of contemplative purgation,[10] when it can find no pleasure, support, consolation or abiding-place in anything soever. Wherefore from this step it begins at once to climb to the second.[11]

2. The second step causes the soul to seek God without ceasing.[12] Wherefore, when the Bride says that she sought Him by night upon her bed (when she had swooned away according to the first step of love) and found Him not, she said: 'I will arise and will seek Him Whom my soul loveth.'[13] This, as we say, the soul does without ceasing, as David counsels it, saying: 'Seek ye ever the face of God, and seek ye Him in all things, tarrying not until ye find Him;'[14] like the Bride, who, having enquired for Him of the watchmen, passed on at once and left them. Mary Magdalene did not even notice the angels at the sepulchre.[15] On this step the soul now walks so anxiously that it seeks the Beloved in all things. In whatsoever it thinks, it thinks at once of the Beloved. Of whatsoever it speaks, in whatsoever matters present themselves, it is speaking and communing at once with the Beloved. When it eats, when it sleeps, when it watches, when it does aught soever, all its care is about the Beloved, as is said above with respect to the yearnings of love. And now, as love begins to recover its health and find new strength in the love of this second step,[16] it begins at once to mount to the third, by means of a certain degree[17] of new purgation in

---

[9] [*Lit.*, 'to enter (upon).']
[10] V: 'of purgative contemplation.'
[11] E.p.: 'to climb to the rest.'
[12] The word 'God' is found only in A, B, e.p.
[13] Canticles iii, 2.
[14] Psalm civ, 4 [A.V., cv, 4].
[15] St. John xx. [This is the reading of all MSS. and editions. The reference is presumably to *v*. 14. But cf. *vv*. 11–13.]
[16] E.p.: '. . . its health, gathering strength on this second step.'
[17] [The word in the Spanish is that elsewhere translated 'step.']

the night, as we shall afterwards describe, which produces in the soul the following effects.

3. The third step of the ladder of love is that which causes the soul to work and gives it fervour so that it fails not. Concerning this the royal Prophet says: 'Blessed is the man that feareth the Lord, for in His commandments he is eager to labour greatly.'[18] Wherefore if fear, being the son of love, causes within him this eagerness to labour,[19] what will be done by love itself? On this step the soul considers great works undertaken for the Beloved as small; many things as few; and the long time for which it serves Him as short, by reason of the fire of love wherein it is now burning. Even so to Jacob, though after seven years he had been made to serve seven more, they seemed few because of the greatness of his love.[20] Now if the love of a mere creature could accomplish so much in Jacob, what will love of the Creator be able to do when on this third step it takes possession of the soul? Here, for the great love which the soul bears to God, it suffers great pains and afflictions because of the little that it does for God; and if it were lawful for it to be destroyed a thousand times for Him it would be comforted. Wherefore it considers itself useless in all that it does and thinks itself to be living in vain. Another wondrous effect produced here in the soul is that it considers itself as being, most certainly, worse than all other souls: first, because love is continually teaching it how much is due to God;[21] and second, because, as the works which it here does for God are many and it knows them all to be faulty and imperfect, they all bring it confusion and affliction, for it realizes in how lowly a manner it is working for God, Who is so high. On this third step, the soul is very far from vainglory or presumption, and from condemning others. These anxious effects, with many others like them, are produced in the soul by this third step;[22] wherefore it[23] gains

[18] Psalm cxi, 1 [A.V., cxii, 1].

[19] [*Lit.*, 'makes in him this labour of eagerness.'] E.p.: 'causes this effect of eagerness.'

[20] Genesis xxix, 20.

[21] [*Lit.*, 'how much God merits.']

[22] E.p. adds: 'of love.'

[23] E.p.: 'wherefore the soul.'

courage and strength from them in order to mount to the fourth step, which is that that follows.

4. The fourth step of this ladder of love is that whereby there is caused in the soul an habitual suffering because of the Beloved, yet without weariness. For, as Saint Augustine says, love makes all things that are great, grievous and burdensome to be almost naught.[24] From this step the Bride was speaking when, desiring to attain to the last step, she said to the Spouse: 'Set me as a seal upon thy heart, as a seal upon thine arm; for love—that is, the act and work of love—is strong as death, and emulation and importunity last as long as hell.'[25] The spirit here has so much strength that it has subjected the flesh and takes as little account of it as does the tree of one of its leaves. In no way does the soul here seek its own consolation or pleasure, either in God, or in aught else, nor does it desire or seek to pray to God for favours, for it sees clearly that it has already received enough of these, and all its anxiety is set upon the manner[26] wherein it will be able to do something that is pleasing to God and to render Him some service such as He merits and in return for what it has received from Him, although it be greatly to its cost. The soul says in its heart and spirit: Ah, my God and Lord! How many are there that go to seek in Thee their own consolation and pleasure, and desire Thee to grant them favours and gifts; but those who long to do Thee pleasure and to give Thee something at their cost, setting their own interests last, are very few. The failure, my God, is not in Thy unwillingness to grant us new favours, but in our neglect to use those that we have received in Thy service alone,[27] in order to constrain Thee to grant them to us continually. Exceeding lofty

[24] E.p. adds: 'and very light.' Cf. St. Augustine: *Serm. IX de Verbis Domini in Evang. secundum Math., in fine:* 'Omnia enim sæva et immania prorsus facilia et prope nulla efficit amor.'

[25] Canticles viii, 5.

[26] E.p.: 'or in aught else, nor from that motive of consolation or self-interest does it beg favours of God. For all its anxiety is now about the manner.'

[27] E.p.: 'For Thou, my God, failest not in willingness to grant us favours; it is we who fail to use those that we have received in Thy service alone.'

is this step of love; for, as the soul goes ever after God with love so true, imbued with the spirit of suffering for His sake, His Majesty oftentimes and quite habitually grants it joy, and visits it sweetly and delectably in the spirit; for the boundless love of Christ, the Word, cannot suffer the afflictions of His lover without succouring him. This He affirmed through Jeremias, saying: 'I have remembered thee, pitying thy youth and tenderness, when thou wentest after Me in the wilderness.'[28] Speaking spiritually, this denotes the detachment which the soul now has interiorly from every creature, so that it rests not and nowhere finds quietness. This fourth step enkindles the soul and makes it to burn in such desire for God that it causes it to mount to the fifth, which is that which follows.

5. The fifth step of this ladder of love makes the soul to desire and long for God impatiently. On this step the vehemence of the lover to comprehend the Beloved and be united with Him is such that every delay, however brief, becomes very long, wearisome and oppressive to it, and it continually believes itself to be finding the Beloved. And when it sees its desire frustrated (which is at almost every moment), it swoons away with its yearning, as says the Psalmist, speaking from this step, in these words: 'My soul longs and faints for the dwellings of the Lord.'[29] On this step the lover must needs see that which he loves, or die; at this step was Rachel,[30] when, for the great longing that she had for children, she said to Jacob, her spouse: 'Give me children, else shall I die.'[31] Here men suffer hunger like dogs and go about and surround the city of God. On this step, which is one of hunger,[32] the soul is nourished upon love; for, even as is its hunger, so is its abundance; so that it rises hence to the sixth step, producing the effects which follow.

[28] Jeremias ii, 2.

[29] Psalm lxxxiii, 2 [A.V., lxxxiv, 2].

[30] E.p.: 'must needs attain that which he loves, or die, even as Rachel,' etc.

[31] Genesis xxx, 1.

[32] [*Lit.*, 'On this hungering step.'] E.p. omits the whole of the preceding sentence and then abbreviates: 'Here the soul is nourished,' etc.

CHAPTER XX

Wherein are treated the other five steps of love.[1]

ON the sixth step the soul runs swiftly to God and touches Him again and again; and it runs without fainting[2] by reason of its hope. For here the love that has made it strong makes it to fly swiftly. Of this step the prophet Isaias speaks thus: 'The saints that hope in God shall renew their strength; they shall take wings as the eagle; they shall fly and shall not faint,'[3] as they did at the fifth step. To this step likewise alludes that verse of the Psalm: 'As the hart desires the waters, my soul desires Thee, O God.'[4] For the hart, in its thirst, runs to the waters with great swiftness. The cause of this swiftness in love which the soul has on this step is that its charity is greatly enlarged[5] within it, since the soul is here almost wholly purified, as is said likewise in the Psalm, namely: *Sine iniquitate cucurri.*[6] And in another Psalm: 'I ran the way of Thy commandments when Thou didst enlarge my heart';[7] and thus from this sixth step the soul at once mounts to the seventh, which is that which follows.

2. The seventh step of this ladder makes the soul to become vehement in its boldness. Here love employs not its judgment in order to hope,[8] nor does it take counsel so that it may draw back, neither can any shame restrain it; for the favour which God here grants to the soul causes it to become vehement in its boldness. Hence follows that which the Apostle says, namely: That charity believeth all things, hopeth

---

[1] So e.p. The Codices make no division.

[2] E.p.: '. . . runs swiftly to God. And thus it runs without fainting.'

[3] Isaias xl, 31. So e.p. The Codices mistakenly attribute this passage to David.

[4] Psalm xli, 2 [A.V., xlii, 1].

[5] V: 'is very delicate' [probably an error: *delicada* for *dilatada*].

[6] Psalm lviii, 5 [A.V., lix, 4].

[7] Psalm cxviii, 32 [A.V., cxix, 32].

[8] E.p.: '. . . in its boldness, and it is carried away thereby with love and intensity, so that it allows not itself to be led away by its judgment in order to hope.'

all things and is capable of all things.[9] Of this step spake Moses, when he entreated God to pardon the people, and if not, to blot out his name from the book of life wherein He had written it.[10] Men like these obtain from God that which they beg of Him with desire. Wherefore David says: 'Delight thou in God and He will give thee the petitions of thy heart.'[11] On this step the Bride grew bold, and said: *Osculetur me osculo oris sui.*[12] To this step it is not lawful[13] for the soul to aspire boldly, unless it feel the interior favour of the King's sceptre extended to it, lest perchance it fall from the other steps which it has mounted up to this point, and wherein it must ever possess itself in humility. From this daring and power which God grants to the soul on this seventh step, so that it may be bold with God in the vehemence of love, follows the eighth, which is that wherein it takes the Beloved captive and is united with Him, as follows.[14]

3. The eighth step of love causes the soul to seize Him and hold Him fast without letting Him go, even as the Bride says, after this manner: 'I found Him Whom my heart and soul love; I held Him and I will not let Him go.'[15] On this step of union the soul satisfies her desire, but not continuously. Certain souls climb some way,[16] and then lose their hold; for, if this state were to continue, it would be glory itself in this life; and thus the soul remains therein[17] for very short periods of time.[18] To the prophet Daniel, because he

---

[9] 1 Corinthians xiii, 7. The sentence 'Hence . . . of all things' is omitted from e.p.

[10] Exodus xxxii, 31-2.

[11] Psalm xxxvi, 4 [A.V., xxxvii, 4].

[12] Canticles i, 1.

[13] E.p.: 'But it is to be emphasized here that it is not lawful,' etc.

[14] E.p. omits: 'as follows.'

[15] Canticles iii, 4.

[16] [*Lit.*, 'attain to setting their foot.']

[17] P: 'walks therein.'

[18] So Bz., H, M, V. P reads as in the preceding note. The other Codices have: 'the soul spends very brief periods of time herein.' E.p. modifies the whole passage thus: 'for, if it were not so, and they remained on this step, they would have a certain kind of glory in this life, and thus the soul spends very short periods of time on this step.'

was a man of desires, was sent a command from God[19] to remain on this step, when it was said to him: 'Daniel, stay upon thy step, because thou art a man of desires.'[20] After this step follows the ninth, which is that of souls now perfect, as we shall afterwards say, which is that that follows.[21]

4. The ninth step of love makes the soul to burn with sweetness. This step is that of the perfect, who now burn sweetly in God. For this sweet and delectable ardour is caused in them by the Holy Spirit by reason of the union which they have with God. For this cause Saint Gregory says, concerning the Apostles, that when the Holy Spirit came upon them visibly they burned inwardly and sweetly through love.[22] Of the good things and riches of God which the soul enjoys on this step, we cannot speak; for if many books were to be written concerning it the greater part would still remain untold. For this cause, and because we shall say something of it hereafter, I say no more here than that after this follows the tenth and last step of this ladder of love, which belongs not to this life.

5. The tenth and last step of this secret ladder of love causes the soul to become wholly assimilated to God, by reason of the clear and immediate[23] vision of God which it then possesses; when, having ascended in this life to the ninth step, it goes forth from the flesh. These souls, who are few, enter not into purgatory, since they have already been wholly purged by love.[24] Of these Saint Matthew says: *Beati mundo corde: quoniam ipsi Deum videbunt.*[25] And, as we say, this vision is the cause of the perfect likeness of the soul to God, for, as Saint John says, we know that we shall be like Him.[26]

[19] E.p.: 'The prophet Daniel . . . was told, on behalf of God,' etc.

[20] Daniel x, 11. E.p. gives the passage in Latin also.

[21] E.p. has only: 'as we shall say.'

[22] 'Dum Deum in ignis visione suscipiunt, per amorem suaviter arserunt' (*Hom. XXX in Evang.*).

[23] [i.e., direct, not mediate.] This adjective is omitted in e.p.

[24] E.p.: 'And these souls, who are few, love is wont to leave completely purged in this life, working that which in the next life is wrought in others by purgatory.'

[25] St. Matthew v, 8.

[26] 1 St. John iii, 2.

Not because the soul will come to have the capacity of God, for that is impossible; but because all that it is will become like to God,[27] for which cause it will be called, and will be, God by participation.

6. This is the secret ladder whereof the soul here speaks, although upon these higher steps it is no longer very secret to the soul, since much is revealed to it by love, through the great effects which love produces in it. But, on this last step of clear vision, which is the last step of the ladder whereon God leans, as we have said already, there is naught that is hidden from the soul, by reason of its complete assimilation. Wherefore Our Saviour says: 'In that day ye shall ask Me nothing,' etc.[28] But, until that day, however high a point the soul may reach, there remains something hidden from it— namely, all that it lacks for total assimilation in the Divine Essence. After this manner, by this mystical theology and secret love, the soul continues to rise above all things and above itself, and to mount upward to God. For love is like fire,[29] which ever rises upward with the desire to be absorbed in the centre of its sphere.

CHAPTER XXI

Which explains the word 'disguised,' and describes the colours of the disguise of the soul in this night.[1]

Now that we have explained the reasons why the soul called this contemplation a 'secret ladder,' it remains for us to explain likewise the word 'disguised,' and the reason why the soul says also that it went forth by this 'secret ladder' in 'disguise.'

2. For the understanding of this it must be known[2] that

[27] E.p. modifies: 'We know that we shall be like Him, for we shall see Him as He is. Wherefore all that [the soul] is will be like to God.'

[28] St. John xvi, 23.

[29] So e.p. The other authorities [and P. Silverio] read: 'is assimilated to fire.'

[1] So e.p. H lacks the first paragraph of this chapter.

[2] E.p.: 'it is necessary to know.'

to disguise oneself is naught else but to hide and cover oneself beneath another garb and figure than one's own—sometimes in order to show forth,[3] under that garb or figure, the
will and purpose which is in the heart to gain the grace and
will of one who is greatly loved; sometimes, again, to hide[4]
oneself from one's rivals and thus to accomplish one's object
better. At such times a man assumes the garments and livery
which best represent and indicate the affection of his heart
and which best conceal him from his rivals.

3. The soul, then, touched with the love of Christ the
Spouse, and longing to attain to His grace and gain His goodwill, goes forth[5] here disguised with that disguise which most
vividly represents the affections of its spirit and which will
protect it most securely on its journey from its adversaries and
enemies, which are the devil, the world and the flesh. Thus
the livery which it wears is of three chief colours—white,
green and purple—denoting the three theological virtues,
faith, hope and charity. By these the soul will not only gain
the grace and goodwill of its Beloved, but it will travel in
security and complete protection from its three enemies: for
faith is an inward tunic of a whiteness so pure that it completely dazzles the eyes of the understanding.[6] And thus,
when the soul journeys in its vestment of faith, the devil can
neither see it nor succeed in harming it, since it is well protected by faith—more so than by all the other virtues[7]—against
the devil, who is at once the strongest and the most cunning
of enemies.

4. It is clear that Saint Peter could find no better protection than faith to save him from the devil, when he said:
Cui resistite fortes in fide.[8] And in order to gain the grace of
the Beloved, and union with Him, the soul cannot put on a
better vest and tunic,[9] to serve as a foundation and beginning

---

[3] E.p. omits 'forth.' [The Spanish phrase has rather the meaning
of 'abroad,' 'to those outside.']

[4] E.p.: 'or to hide.'

[5] E.p.: 'of Christ its Spouse, because it longs . . . goes forth.'

[6] [*Lit.*, 'that it dislocates the sight of all understanding.']

[7] E p. omits: 'more . . . virtues.'

[8] 1 St. Peter v, 9.

[9] [*Lit.*, 'a better undershirt and tunic.']

of the other vestments of the virtues, than this white garment[10] of faith, for without it, as the Apostle says, it is impossible to please God, and with it, it is impossible to fail to please Him.[11] For He Himself says through a prophet: *Sponsabo te mihi in fide*.[12] Which is as much as to say: If thou desirest, O soul, to be united and betrothed to Me, thou must come inwardly clad in faith.

5. This white garment of faith was worn by the soul on its going forth from this dark night, when, walking in interior constraint and darkness, as we have said before, it received no aid, in the form of light, from its understanding, neither from above, since Heaven seemed to be closed to it and God hidden from it, nor from below, since those that taught it satisfied it not. It suffered with constancy and persevered, passing through those trials without fainting or failing the Beloved, Who in trials and tribulations proves the faith of His Bride, so that afterwards she may truly repeat this saying of David, namely: 'By the words of Thy lips I kept hard ways.'[13]

6. Next, over this white tunic of faith the soul now puts on the second colour, which is a green vestment.[14] By this, as we said, is signified[15] the virtue of hope, wherewith, as in the first case, the soul is delivered and protected from the second enemy, which is the world. For this green colour of living hope in God gives the soul such ardour and courage and aspiration to the things of eternal life that, by comparison with what it hopes for therein, all things of the world seem to it to be, as in truth they are, dry and faded and dead and nothing worth. The soul now divests and strips itself of all these worldly vestments and garments, setting its heart upon naught that is in the world and hoping for naught, whether of that which is or of that which is to be, but living clad only in the hope of eternal life. Wherefore, when the

---

[10] [*Lit.*, 'this whiteness.']

[11] A adds: 'if it be [a] living [faith].' E.p.: 'and with it, if it be [a] living [faith], it pleases Him and seems well to Him.'

[12] Osee ii, 20.

[13] Psalm xvi, 4 [A.V., xvii, 4].

[14] So e.p., substituting this more general word for the *almilla* [a kind of under-waistcoat] of the Codices.

[15] E.p.: 'By the which colour is signified.'

heart is thus lifted up above the world, not only can the world neither touch the heart[16] nor lay hold on it, but it cannot even come within sight of it.

7. And thus, in this green livery and disguise, the soul journeys in complete security from this second enemy, which is the world. For Saint Paul speaks of hope as the helmet of salvation[17]—that is, a piece of armour that protects the whole head, and covers it so that there remains uncovered only a visor through which it may look. And hope has this property, that it covers all the senses of the head of the soul, so that there is naught soever pertaining to the world in which they can be immersed, nor is there an opening through which any arrow of the world[18] can wound them. It has a visor, however, which the soul is permitted to use so that its eyes may look upward, but nowhere else; for this is the function which hope habitually performs in the soul, namely, the directing of its eyes upwards to look at God alone, even as David declared that his eyes were directed, when he said:[19] *Oculi mei semper ad Dominum.*[20] He hoped for no good thing elsewhere, save as he himself says in another Psalm: 'Even as the eyes of the handmaid are set upon the hands of her mistress, even so are our eyes set upon our Lord God, until He have mercy upon us as we hope in Him.'[21]

8. For this reason,[22] because of this green livery (since the soul is ever looking to God and sets its eyes on naught else, neither is pleased with aught save with Him alone), the Beloved has such great pleasure with the soul that it is true to say that the soul obtains from Him as much as it hopes for from Him. Wherefore the Spouse[23] in the Songs tells the Bride that, by looking upon Him with one eye alone, she has wounded His heart.[24] Without this green livery of hope in

[16] E.p.: 'touch it.'
[17] 1 Thessalonians v, 8.
[18] E.p.: 'any arrow thereof.'
[19] E.p. abbreviates: 'even as David says.'
[20] Psalm xxiv, 15 [A.V., xxv, 15].
[21] Psalm cxxii, 2 [A.V., cxxiii, 2].
[22] E.p. omits: 'For this reason.'
[23] E.p.: 'Wherefore He.'
[24] Canticles iv, 9.

God alone it would be impossible for the soul to go forth to encompass this loving achievement, for it would have no success, since that which moves and conquers is the importunity of hope.

9. With this livery of hope the soul journeys in disguise through this secret and dark night whereof we have spoken;[25] for it is so completely voided of every possession and support that it fixes its eyes and its care upon naught but God, putting its mouth in the dust,[26] if so be there may be hope—to repeat the quotation made above from Jeremias.[27]

10. Over the white and the green vestments, as the crown and perfection of this disguise and livery, the soul now puts on the third colour, which is a splendid garment of purple. By this is denoted the third virtue, which is charity. This not only adds grace to the other two colours, but causes the soul to rise to so lofty a point that it is brought near to God, and becomes very beautiful and pleasing to Him, so that it makes bold to say: 'Albeit I am black, O daughters of Jerusalem, I am comely; wherefore the King hath loved me and hath brought me into His chambers.'[28] This livery of charity, which is that of love, and causes greater love in the Beloved,[29] not only protects the soul and hides it from the third enemy, which is the flesh (for where there is true love of God there enters neither love of self nor that of the things of self), but even gives worth to the other virtues, bestowing on them vigour and strength to protect the soul, and grace and beauty to please the Beloved with them, for without charity no virtue has grace before God. This is the purple which is spoken of in the Songs,[30] upon which God reclines.[31] Clad in this purple livery the soul journeys when (as has been explained above in

[25] E.p. omits: 'whereof we have spoken.'

[26] Lamentations iii, 29.

[27] *Ibid*. [For the quotation, see Bk. II, chap. viii, § 1, p. 115, above.]

[28] Canticles i, 3. [A.V., i, 4.] [For 'chambers' the Spanish has 'bed.']

[29] E.p. omits: 'and . . . Beloved.'

[30] Canticles iii, 10.

[31] Some authorities add: 'whereby He goes up to the reclining-place.'

the first stanza) it goes forth from itself in the dark night, and from all things created, 'kindled in love with yearnings,' by this secret ladder of contemplation, to the perfect union of love of God, its beloved salvation.[32]

11. This, then, is the disguise which the soul says that it wears in the night of faith, upon this secret ladder, and these are its three colours. They constitute a most fit preparation for the union of the soul with God, according to its three faculties, which are understanding, memory and will. For faith voids and darkens the understanding as to all its natural intelligence, and herein prepares it for union with Divine Wisdom. Hope voids and withdraws the memory from all creature possessions; for, as Saint Paul says, hope is for that which is not possessed;[33] and thus it withdraws the memory from that which it is capable of possessing,[34] and sets it on that for which it hopes.[35] And for this cause hope in God alone prepares the memory purely for union with God.[36] Charity, in the same way, voids and annihilates the affections and desires of the will for whatever is not God, and sets them upon Him alone; and thus this virtue prepares this faculty and unites it with God through love. And thus,[37] since the function of these virtues is the withdrawal of the soul from all that is less than God, their function is consequently that of joining it with God.

12. And thus, unless it journeys earnestly, clad in the garments of these three virtues, it is impossible for the soul to attain to the perfection of union with God through love.[38] Wherefore, in order that the soul might attain that which it desired, which was this loving and delectable union with its Beloved, this disguise and clothing which it assumed was most necessary and convenient. And likewise to have succeeded in thus clothing itself and persevering until it should

[32] [Or 'health.']

[33] Romans viii, 24.

[34] E.p. adds: 'in this life.'

[35] E.p.: 'on that which it hopes to possess.'

[36] E.p. substitutes for 'for union with God' 'according to the void caused in it that it may be united with Him.'

[37] E.p.: 'Wherefore.'

[38] E.p.: 'to the perfection of love with God.'

obtain the end and aspiration which it had so much desired, which was the union of love, was a great and happy chance, wherefore in this line the soul also says:

Oh, happy chance!

CHAPTER XXII

Explains the third[1] line of the second stanza.[2]

It is very clear that it was a happy chance for this soul to go forth with such an enterprise as this, for it was its going forth that delivered it[3] from the devil and from the world and from its own sensuality, as we have said.[4] Having attained liberty of spirit, so precious[5] and so greatly desired by all, it went forth from low things to high; from terrestrial, it became celestial; from human, Divine. Thus it came to have its conversation in the heavens, as has the soul in this state of perfection, even as we shall go on to say in what follows,[6] although with rather more brevity.

2. For the most important part of my task, and the part which chiefly led me to undertake it, was the explanation of this night to many souls who pass through it and yet know nothing about it, as was said in the prologue. Now this explanation and exposition has already been half completed. Although much less has been said of it than might be said, we have shown how many are the blessings which the soul bears with it through the night and how happy is the chance whereby it passes through it, so that, when a soul is terrified by the horror of so many trials, it is also encouraged by the certain hope of so many and such precious blessings of God as it gains therein. And furthermore, for yet another reason,

---

[1] i.e., in the original Spanish and in our verse rendering of the poem in *The Complete Works of St. John of the Cross*, Ed. by E. Allison Peers, Vol. II (The Newman Press, Westminster, Md.).

[2] So e.p. The Codices make no division.

[3] E.p. has [for 'for it . . . it'] 'wherein it was delivered.'

[4] E.p. omits: 'as we have said.'

[5] H has 'happy' for 'precious.'

[6] E.p. omits: 'in what follows.'

this was a happy chance for the soul; and this reason is given in the following line:

In darkness and in concealment.

CHAPTER XXIII

Expounds the fourth line[1] and describes the wondrous hiding-place wherein the soul is set during this night. Shows how, although the devil has an entrance into other places that are very high, he has none into this.[2]

'IN concealment' is as much as to say 'in a hiding-place,' or 'in hiding'; and thus, what the soul here says (namely,[3] that it went forth 'in darkness and in concealment') is a more complete explanation of the great security which it describes itself in the first line of the stanza as possessing, by means of this dark contemplation upon the road of the union of the love of God.

2. When the soul, then, says 'in darkness and in conceal-ment,' it means that, inasmuch as it journeyed in darkness after the manner aforementioned, it went in hiding and in concealment from the devil and from his wiles and stratagems. The reason why, as it journeys in the darkness of this con-templation, the soul is free, and is hidden from the stratagems of the devil, is that the infused contemplation which it here possesses is infused into it passively and secretly, without the knowledge of[4] the senses and faculties, whether interior or exterior, of the sensual part. And hence it follows that, not only does it journey in hiding, and is free from the impedi-ment which these faculties can set in its way because of its natural weakness, but likewise from the devil; who, except through these faculties of the sensual part, cannot reach or know that which is in the soul, nor that which is taking place

---

[1] i.e., in the original Spanish and in our verse rendering of the poem in *The Complete Works of St. John of the Cross,* Ed. by E. Allison Peers, Vol. II (The Newman Press, Westminster, Md.).

[2] So e.p. The Codices make no division.

[3] E.p. omits 'namely.'

[4] A, B, C, V: 'concealed by the darkness from.'

within it. Wherefore, the more spiritual, the more interior
and the more remote from the senses is the communication,
the farther does the devil fall short of understanding it.

3. And thus it is of great importance for the security of the
soul that its inward communication with God should be of
such a kind that its very senses of the lower part will remain
in darkness[5] and be without knowledge of it, and attain not
to it: first, so that it may be possible for the spiritual communication to be more abundant, and that the weakness of
its sensual part may not hinder the liberty of its spirit; secondly because, as we say, the soul journeys more securely
since the devil cannot penetrate so far. In this way we may
understand that passage where Our Saviour, speaking in a
spiritual sense, says: 'Let not thy left hand know what thy
right hand doeth.'[6] Which is as though He had said: Let not
thy left hand know that which takes place upon thy right
hand, which is the higher and spiritual part of the soul;
that is, let it be of such a kind that the lower portion of thy
soul, which is the sensual part, may not attain to it; let it be
a secret between the spirit and God alone.

4. It is quite true that oftentimes, when these very intimate and secret spiritual communications are present and take
place in the soul, although the devil cannot get to know of
what kind and manner they are, yet the great repose and
silence which some of them cause in the senses and the
faculties of the sensual part make it clear to him that they are
taking place and that the soul is receiving a certain blessing[7]
from them. And then, as he sees that he cannot succeed in
thwarting them in the depth of the soul, he does what he can
to disturb and disquiet the sensual part—that part to which
he is able to attain—now by means of afflictions, now by
terrors and fears, with intent to disquiet and disturb the
higher and spiritual part of the soul by this means, with
respect to that blessing which it then receives and enjoys.
But often, when the communication of such contemplation

[5] [The Spanish also admits of the rendering: 'remain shut off
from it by darkness.']
[6] St. Matthew vi, 3.
[7] E.p.: 'a certain great blessing.'

makes its naked assault upon the soul and exerts its strength
upon it, the devil, with all his diligence, is unable to disturb
it; rather the soul receives a new and a greater advantage[8]
and a securer peace. For, when it feels the disturbing presence
of the enemy, then—wondrous thing!—without knowing
how it comes to pass, and without any efforts of its own,[9] it
enters farther into its own interior depths, feeling that it is
indeed being set in a sure refuge, where it perceives itself to
be most completely withdrawn and hidden from the enemy.
And thus its peace and joy, which the devil is attempting to
take from it, are increased; and all the fear that assails it
remains without; and it becomes clearly and exultingly conscious of its secure enjoyment of that quiet peace and sweetness of the hidden Spouse,[10] which neither the world nor the
devil can give it or take from it. In that state, therefore, it
realizes the truth of the words of the Bride about this, in the
Songs, namely: 'See how threescore strong men surround the
bed of Solomon, etc., because of the fears of the night.'[11] It
is conscious of this strength and peace, although it is often
equally conscious that its flesh and bones are being tormented
from without.

5. At other times, when the spiritual communication is
not made in any great measure to the spirit, but the senses
have a part therein,[12] the devil more easily succeeds in disturbing the spirit and raising a tumult within it, by means of
the senses, with these terrors. Great are the torment and the
affliction which are then caused in the spirit; at times they
exceed all that can be expressed. For, when there is a naked
contact of spirit with spirit, the horror is intolerable which
the evil spirit causes in the good spirit (I mean, in the soul),
when its tumult reaches it. This is expressed likewise by the
Bride in the Songs, when she says that it has happened thus
to her at a time when she wished to descend to interior
recollection in order to have fruition of these blessings. She

---

[8] E.p.: 'a new advantage and love.'
[9] E.p. omits: 'and without any efforts of its own.'
[10] E.p.: 'of the Spouse in hiding.'
[11] Canticles iii, 7–8.
[12] E.p.: 'is accompanied by [communications to] sense.'

says: 'I went down into the garden of nuts to see the apples of the valleys, and if the vine had flourished. I knew not; my soul troubled me because of the chariots'—that is, because of the chariots and the noise of Aminadab, which is the devil.[13]

6. At other times it comes to pass that the devil is occasionally able to see certain favours which God is pleased to grant the soul when they are bestowed upon it by the mediation of a good angel; for of those favours which come through a good angel God habitually allows the enemy to have knowledge[14]: partly so that he may do that which he can against them according to the measure of justice, and that thus he may not be able to allege with truth that no opportunity is given him for conquering the soul, as he said concerning Job.[15] This would be the case if God allowed not a certain equality between the two warriors—namely, the good angel and the bad—when they strive for the soul, so that the victory of either may be of the greater worth[16] and the soul that is victorious and faithful in temptation may be the more abundantly rewarded.

7. We must observe, therefore, that it is for this reason that, in proportion as God is guiding the soul and communing with it, He gives the devil leave to act with it after this manner. When the soul has genuine visions by the instrumentality of the good angel (for it is by this instrumentality that they habitually come, even though Christ reveal Himself, for He scarcely ever appears[17] in His actual person),

---

[13] Canticles vi, 10 [A.V., vi, 11–12].

[14] E.p.: 'At other times this opposition of the devil takes place when God grants favours to the soul by the mediation of a good angel; for these [favours] the devil is occasionally able to see because God habitually allows the enemy to have knowledge of them.'

[15] Job i, 1–11.

[16] E.p. substitutes for this sentence: 'And thus it is meet that God should allow a certain equality between the two warriors—namely, the good angel and the bad—when they strive for the soul, that the victory may be of the greater worth.'

[17] Such is the unanimous opinion of theologians. Some, with St. Thomas (Pt. III, q. 57, a. 6), suppose that the appearance which converted St. Paul near Damascus was that of Our Lord Jesus Christ in person.

God also gives[18] the wicked angel leave to present to the soul false visions of this very type in such a way that the soul which is not cautious may easily be deceived by their outward appearance, as many souls have been. Of this there is a figure in Exodus,[19] where it is said that all the genuine signs that Moses wrought were wrought likewise in appearance by the magicians of Pharao. If he brought forth frogs, they brought them forth likewise; if he turned water into blood, they did the same.

8. And not only does the evil one imitate God in this type of bodily vision, but he also imitates and interferes in spiritual communications which come through the instrumentality of an angel, when he succeeds in seeing them, as we say (for, as Job said[20]: *Omne sublime videt*). These, however, as they are without form and figure (for it is the nature of spirit to have no such thing), he cannot imitate and counterfeit like those others which are presented under some species or figure. And thus, in order to attack the soul, in the same way as that wherein it is being visited, his fearful spirit presents a similar vision in order to attack and destroy spiritual things by spiritual. When this comes to pass just as the good angel is about to communicate spiritual contemplation to the soul, it is impossible for the soul to shelter itself in the secrecy and hiding-place of contemplation with sufficient rapidity not to be observed by the devil; and thus he appears to it and produces a certain horror and perturbation of spirit[21] which at times is most distressing to the soul. Sometimes the soul can speedily free itself from him, so that there is no opportunity for the aforementioned horror of the evil spirit to make an

---

[18] E.p. modifies: '. . . for this reason that, at certain times, in that order whereby God is leading the soul, He gives leave to the devil to disquiet and tempt it, as happens when it has genuine visions by the instrumentality of a good angel, and God also gives,' etc.

[19] Exodus vii, 11–22; viii, 7.

[20] Job xli, 25. E.p. modifies: '. . . of an angel, when he succeeds in seeing them; since, as Job said,' etc.

[21] E.p. abbreviates: 'his fearful spirit presents it [i.e., the vision] as it can, when the good angel is about to communicate to the soul spiritual contemplation, and produces a certain horror and perturbation of spirit.'

impression on it; and it becomes recollected within itself, being favoured, to this end, by the effectual spiritual grace that the good angel then communicates to it.

9. At other times the devil prevails and encompasses the soul with a perturbation and horror which is a greater affliction to it than any torment in this life could be. For, as this horrible communication passes direct from spirit to spirit, in something like nakedness and clearly distinguished from all that is corporeal, it is grievous beyond what every sense can feel; and this lasts in the spirit for some time, yet not for long, for otherwise the spirit would be driven forth from the flesh by the vehement communication of the other spirit. Afterwards there remains to it the memory thereof, which is sufficient to cause it great affliction.[22]

10. All that we have here described comes to pass in the soul passively, without its doing or undoing anything of itself with respect to it.[23] But in this connection it must be known that, when the good angel permits the devil to gain this advantage of assailing the soul[24] with this spiritual horror, he does it to purify the soul and to prepare it by means of this spiritual vigil for some great spiritual favour and festival which he desires to grant it, for he never mortifies save to give life, nor humbles save to exalt, which comes to pass shortly afterwards. Then, according as was the dark and horrible[25] purgation which the soul suffered, so is the fruition now granted it of a wondrous and delectable spiritual contemplation,[26] sometimes so lofty that there is no language to describe it.[27] But the spirit has been greatly refined by the preceding horror of the evil spirit, in order that it may

[22] E.p. abbreviates: 'At other times God allows this perturbation and horror to last longer, which is a greater affliction to the soul than any torment in this life could be. And afterwards there remains to it the memory thereof, which is sufficient to cause it great affliction.'

[23] E.p.: 'All that we have said comes to pass in the soul without its doing or undoing anything of itself with respect to this representation or feeling.'

[24] E.p.: 'when God permits the devil thus to afflict the soul.'

[25] E.p. omits: 'and horrible.'

[26] E.p. omits: 'wondrous and.'

[27] The remainder of this paragraph is omitted in e.p.

be able to receive this blessing; for these spiritual visions belong to the next life rather than to this, and when one of them is seen this is a preparation for the next.

11. This is to be understood with respect to occasions when God visits the soul by the instrumentality of a good angel, wherein, as has been said, the soul is not so totally[28] in darkness and in concealment that the enemy cannot come within reach of it. But, when God Himself visits it, then the words of this line are indeed fulfilled, and it is in total darkness and in concealment from the enemy that the soul receives these spiritual favours of God. The reason for this is that, as His Majesty dwells[29] substantially in the soul, where neither angel nor devil can attain to an understanding of that which comes to pass, they cannot know the intimate and secret communications which take place there between the soul and God. These communications, since the Lord Himself works them, are wholly Divine and sovereign, for they are all substantial touches[30] of Divine union between the soul and God; in one of which the soul receives a greater blessing than in all the rest, since this is the loftiest degree[31] of prayer in existence.

12. For these are the touches that the Bride entreated of Him in the Songs, saying: *Osculetur me osculo oris sui*.[32] Since this is a thing which takes place in such close intimacy with God, whereto the soul desires with such yearnings to attain, it esteems and longs for a touch of this Divinity more than all the other favours that God grants it. Wherefore, after many such favours have been granted to the Bride in the said Songs, of which she has sung therein, she is not satisfied, but entreats Him for these Divine touches, saying: 'Who shall give Thee to me, my brother, that I might find Thee alone without, sucking the breasts of my mother, so that I might kiss Thee with the mouth of my soul, and that thus no man should despise me or make bold to attack me.'[33] By this

---

[28] E.p.: 'the soul is [*lit.*, goes] not secure, nor is so totally.'
[29] E.p.: 'as His Majesty is the supreme Lord and dwells.'
[30] E.p.: 'and, as it were, touches.'
[31] [*Lit.*, 'step.' Cf. p. 167, n. 1, above.]
[32] Canticles i, 1.
[33] Canticles viii, 1.

she denotes the communication which God Himself alone makes to her, as we are saying,[34] far from all the creatures and without their knowledge,[35] for this is meant by 'alone and without, sucking, etc.'[36]—that is, drying up and draining the breasts of the desires and affections of the sensual part of the soul. This takes place when the soul, in intimate peace and delight, has fruition of these blessings, with liberty of spirit, and without the sensual part being able to hinder it, or the devil to thwart it by means thereof. And then the devil would not make bold to attack it, for he would not reach it, neither could he attain to an understanding of these Divine touches in the substance of the soul in[37] the loving substance of God.

13. To this blessing none attains save through intimate purgation and detachment and spiritual concealment from all that is creature; it comes to pass in the darkness, as we have already explained at length and as we say with respect to this line. The soul is in concealment and in hiding, in the which hiding-place, as we have now said, it continues to be strengthened[38] in union with God through love, wherefore it sings this in the same phrase, saying: 'In darkness and in concealment.'

14. When it comes to pass that those favours are granted to the soul in concealment (that is, as we have said, in spirit only), the soul is wont, during some of them, and without knowing how this comes to pass, to see itself so far withdrawn and separated[39] according to the higher and spiritual part, from the sensual and lower portion,[40] that it recognizes in itself two parts so distinct from each other that it believes that the one has naught to do with the other, but that the one is very remote and far withdrawn from the other. And in reality, in a certain way, this is so; for the operation is now

[34] E.p. omits: 'as we are saying.'

[35] B, C, M, Mtr., V have: 'and concealed from them by darkness.'

[36] The remainder of this sentence is omitted in e.p.

[37] E.p.: 'with.'

[38] E.p. shortens this sentence thus: 'This is in darkness, in the which hiding-place the soul continues to be strengthened,' etc.

[39] E.p.: 'so far separated.'

[40] E.p.: 'according to the higher part, from the lower portion.'

wholly spiritual,[41] and the soul receives no communication in its sensual part. In this way the soul gradually becomes wholly spiritual; and in this hiding-place of unitive contemplation its spiritual desires and passions are to a great degree removed and purged away. And thus, speaking of its higher part, the soul then says in this last line:

My house being now at rest.[42]

CHAPTER XXIV

Completes the explanation of the second stanza.[1]

THIS is as much as to say: The higher portion of my soul being like the lower part also, at rest with respect to its desires and faculties, I went forth to the Divine union of the love of God.

2. Inasmuch as, by means of that war of the dark night, as has been said, the soul is combated[2] and purged after two manners—namely, according to its sensual and its spiritual part—with its senses, faculties and passions, so likewise after two manners—namely,[3] according to these two parts, the sensual and the spiritual—with all its faculties and desires, the soul attains to an enjoyment of peace and rest. For this reason, as has likewise been said, the soul twice pronounces this line—namely,[4] in this stanza and in the last—because of these two portions of the soul, the spiritual and the sensual, which, in order that they may go forth to the Divine union of love, must needs first be reformed, ordered and tranquillized[5] with respect to the sensual and to the spiritual, according to the nature of the state of innocence which was Adam's.[6]

[41] A, B, e.p.: 'the operation which now works is wholly spiritual.'
[42] The word translated 'at rest' is a past participle: more literally, 'stilled.'

[1] From e.p.
[2] Bz. has: 'is converted'; [perhaps] in error.
[3] E.p. omits 'namely.'
[4] [*Lit.*, 'twice repeats'—a loosely used phrase.] E.p. omits 'namely.'
[5] Bz. reads: 'and taken away' [*quitadas* for *quietas*], an error.
[6] H omits this last phrase, which is found in all the other Codices, and in e.p. The latter adds: 'notwithstanding that the soul is not

And thus this line which, in the first stanza, was understood of the repose of the lower and sensual portion,[7] is, in this second stanza, understood more particularly of the higher and spiritual part; for which reason it is repeated.[8]

3. This repose and quiet of this spiritual house the soul comes to attain, habitually and perfectly (in so far as the condition of this life allows), by means of the acts of the substantial touches[9] of Divine union whereof we have just spoken; which, in concealment, and hidden from the perturbation of the devil, and of its own senses and passions, the soul has been receiving from the Divinity, wherein it has been purifying itself, as I say, resting, strengthening and confirming itself in order to be able to receive the said union once and for all, which is the Divine betrothal between the soul and the Son of God. As soon as these two houses of the soul have together become tranquillized and strengthened, with all their domestics—namely, the faculties and desires— and have put these domestics to sleep and made them to be silent with respect to all things, both above and below, this Divine Wisdom immediately unites itself with the soul by making a new bond of loving possession, and there is fulfilled that which is written in the Book of Wisdom, in these words:[10] *Dum quietum silentium contineret omnia, et nox in suo cursu medium iter haberet, omnipotens sermo tuus Domine a regalibus sedibus.*[11] The same thing is described by the Bride

---

wholly free from the temptations of the lower part.' The addition is made so that the teaching of the Saint may not be confused with that of the Illuminists, who supposed the contemplative in union to be impeccable, do what he might. The Saint's meaning is that for the mystical union of the soul with God such purity and tranquillity of senses and faculties are needful that his condition resembles that state of innocence in which Adam was created, but without the attribute of impeccability, which does not necessarily accompany union, nor can be attained by any, save by a most special privilege of God. Cf. St. Teresa's *Interior Castle*, VII, ii. St. Teresa will be found occasionally to explain points of mystical doctrine which St. John of the Cross takes as being understood.

[7] E.p.: 'part' for 'portion.'
[8] [*Lit.*, 'twice repeated.']
[9] E.p.: 'of these (as it were) substantial touches.'
[10] E.p.: 'that which it [i.e., Wisdom] says.'
[11] Wisdom xviii, 14.

in the Songs,[12] where she says that, after she had passed by those who stripped her of her mantle by night and wounded her, she found Him Whom her soul loved.

4. The soul cannot come to this union without great purity, and this purity is not gained without great detachment from every created thing and sharp mortification. This is signified by the stripping of the Bride of her mantle and by her being wounded by night as she sought and went after the Spouse; for the new mantle which belonged to the betrothal could not be put on until the old mantle was stripped off. Wherefore, he that refuses to go forth in the night aforementioned to seek the Beloved, and to be stripped of his own will and to be mortified, but seeks Him upon his bed and at his own convenience, as did the Bride,[13] will not succeed in finding Him. For this soul says of itself that it found Him by going forth in the dark and with yearnings of love.

CHAPTER XXV

Wherein is expounded the third stanza.[1]

In the happy night, In secret, when none saw me, Nor I beheld aught, Without light or guide, save that which burned in my heart.

EXPOSITION

THE soul still continues the metaphor and similitude of temporal night in describing this its spiritual night, and continues to sing and extol the good properties which belong to it, and which in passing through this night it found and used, to the end that it might attain its desired goal with speed and security. Of these properties it here sets down three.

2. The first, it says, is that in this happy night of con-

[12] Canticles v, 7.
[13] Canticles iii, 1.
[1] From e.p. Some of the Codices have 'Stanza the Third' and some simply 'Stanza.' Bz., P omit the whole chapter.

templation God leads the soul by a manner of contemplation so solitary and secret, so remote and far distant from sense, that naught pertaining to it, nor any touch of created things, succeeds in approaching the soul in such a way as to disturb it and detain it on the road of the union of love.

3. The second property whereof it speaks pertains to the spiritual darkness of this night, wherein all the faculties of the higher part of the soul are in darkness. The soul sees naught, neither looks at aught neither stays in aught that is not God, to the end that it may reach Him, inasmuch as it journeys unimpeded by obstacles of forms and figures, and of natural apprehensions, which are those that are wont to hinder the soul from uniting with the eternal Being of God.[2]

4. The third is that, although as it journeys it is supported by no particular interior light of understanding, nor by any exterior guide, that it may receive satisfaction therefrom on this lofty road—it is completely deprived of all this by this thick darkness—yet its love alone, which burns[3] at this time, and makes its heart to long for the Beloved, is that which now moves and guides it, and makes it to soar upward to its God along the road of solitude, without its knowing how or in what manner.

There follows the line:

In the happy night.[4]

[2] So G, H, Mtr. [Lit., 'that it may not unite itself in the ever being of God.' Siempre, 'ever,' 'always,' is normally an adverb.] A, B have: 'that it may not unite itself always and be with God.' C, M, e.p.: 'that it may not unite itself always with God.'

[3] E.p.: 'but it is love and faith which burn.'

[4] Thus end the majority of the MSS. Cf. pp. lviii–lxiii, Ascent of Mount Carmel (Image Books edition), 26–27, above, on the incomplete state of this treatise. The MSS. say nothing of this, except that in the Alba de Tormes MS. we read: 'Thus far wrote the holy Fray John of the Cross concerning the purgative way, wherein he treats of the active and the passive [aspect] of it as is seen in the treatise of the Ascent of the Mount and in this of the Dark Night, and, as he died, he wrote no more. And hereafter follows the illuminative way, and then the unitive.' Elsewhere we have said that the lack of any commentary on the last five stanzas is not due to the Saint's death, since he lived for many years after writing the commentary on the earlier stanzas.

OTHER IMAGE BOOKS

THE IMITATION OF CHRIST – Thomas à Kempis. Edited with an Introduction by Harold C. Gardiner, S.J. (D17) – $1.25

ST. FRANCIS OF ASSISI – G. K. Chesterton (D50) – $1.25

VIPER'S TANGLE – François Mauriac. A novel of evil and redemption (D51) – 95¢

THE CITY OF GOD – St. Augustine. Edited by Vernon J. Bourke. Introduction by Étienne Gilson. Specially abridged (D59) – $2.45

RELIGION AND THE RISE OF WESTERN CULTURE – Christopher Dawson (D64) – $1.25

JESUS AND HIS TIMES – Henri Daniel-Rops (D67b) – $1.25

THE LITTLE FLOWERS OF ST. FRANCIS – Translated by Raphael Brown (D69) – $1.75

THE IDEA OF A UNIVERSITY – John Henry Cardinal Newman. Introduction by G. N. Shuster (D75) – $1.65

DARK NIGHT OF THE SOUL – St. John of the Cross. Edited and translated by E. Allison Peers (D78) – $1.25

THE PILLAR OF FIRE – Karl Stern. A psychiatrist's spiritual journey from Judaism to Catholicism (D83) – 95¢

A POPULAR HISTORY OF THE REFORMATION – Philip Hughes (D92) – $1.25

THE CONFESSIONS OF ST. AUGUSTINE – Translated with an Introduction by John K. Ryan (D101) – $1.75

THE THIRD REVOLUTION: A Study of Psychiatry and Religion – Dr. Karl Stern (D113) – 95¢

A HISTORY OF PHILOSOPHY: VOLUME 1 – GREECE AND ROME (2 Parts) – Frederick Copleston, S.J. (D134a, D134b) – $1.75 ea.

A HISTORY OF PHILOSOPHY: VOLUME 2 – MEDIAEVAL PHILOSOPHY (2 Parts) – Frederick Copleston, S.J. Part I – Augustine to Bonaventure. Part II – Albert the Great to Duns Scotus (D135a, D135b) – $1.45 ea.

A HISTORY OF PHILOSOPHY: VOLUME 3 – LATE MEDIAEVAL AND RENAISSANCE PHILOSOPHY (2 Parts) – Frederick Copleston, S.J. Part I – Ockham to the Speculative Mystics. Part II – The Revival of Platonism to Suárez (D136a, D136b) – $1.45 ea.

A HISTORY OF PHILOSOPHY: VOLUME 4 – MODERN PHILOSOPHY: Descartes to Leibniz – Frederick Copleston, S.J. (D137) – $1.75

OTHER IMAGE BOOKS

OTHER IMAGE BOOKS

OTHER IMAGE BOOKS

B 72 – 4